WESTERN

Trees

A FIELD GUIDE

Text by Maggie Stuckey and George Palmer
Illustrations: Keith Bowers
Technical Editor: Ken Bierly

FALCON®

Helena, Montana

Editing, design, typesetting, and other prepress work by Falcon® Publishing, Inc.,
Helena, Montana.
Binding and printing in the United States of America

Library of Congress Cataloging-in-Publication data:

Stuckey, Maggie.
    Western trees: a field guide / text by Maggie Stuckey and George
Palmer ; illustrations by Keith Bowers ; technical editor, Ken
Bierly.
        p. cm.
    Rev. ed. of : Western treebook / George Palmer, Martha Stuckey.
    c1977.
    Includes bibliographical references.
    ISBN 1-56044-623-4 (paperback)
    1. Trees--West (U.S.)--Identification. I. Palmer, George, 1939-
. II. Palmer, George, 1939- Western treebook. III. Title.
    QK133.S78 1998
    582.16' 0978--dc21

For extra copies of this book please check with your local bookstore,
or write Falcon, P. O. Box 1718, Helena, MT 59624.
You may also call toll-free 1-800-582-2665, or to contact us via e-mail, visit our homepage
on the world wide web at http://www.falconguide.com

WESTERN TREES:
A FIELD GUIDE

At the gates of the forest, the surprised man of the world is forced to leave his city estimates of great and small, wise and foolish.

Ralph Waldo Emerson

Geographic Range

Contents

Any fool can destroy trees. During a man's life only saplings can be grown, in the place of the old trees—tens of centuries old—that have been destroyed. It took more than three thousand years to make some of the trees in these Western woods—trees that are still standing in perfect strength and beauty, waving and singing. Through all the wonderful, eventful centuries since Christ's time—and long before that—God has cared for these trees, saved them from drought, disease, avalanche, and a thousand straining, leveling tempests and floods; but he cannot save them from fools.

John Muir

Introduction
How This Book Came Into Being

How does a book originate? In this case, we simply got mad. We love the outdoors and try to spend as much time as possible in the forest, backpacking, picnicking or just hiking for pleasure. We are curious backcountry travelers, wanting to find out more about what kinds of things are where, how they got there, and what role they play in the scheme of things. That means taking along some good reference books. But we are also lazy, and will go to almost any extreme to trim ounces from our loads, without inhibiting our capacity to learn from the books we take along. So we are on a constant search for just the *right* books. Tree books have always been a particular source of frustration. The books we had to work with covered too broad a range, or too narrow, or were too cumbersome to use, or too technically oriented, or gave us too little information: only the name, but nothing about the tree.

"What we need," we often said, "is a book for ordinary, curious people." And so we ended up writing one. Our goal was to compile a book which is both interesting and easy to use. We wanted to include more than just a tree's name and botanical description, but also its habits, its uses, both present and past, and any unique ecological characteristics. We felt the book should include the trees which ordinary folks would be likely to encounter on an average trip in the Western states. We wanted it to fit into a daypack or a large pocket, and not weigh too much.

Above all, we wanted a book that people could actually *use*. We tried to devise ways to organize and present the material that would increase the book's "use-ability." The Leaf Key, the comparison charts for look-alike trees, the measuring devices based on the size of the book itself. . . these and other features grew out of our desire to make a truly useful fieldbook.

If you find convenience in using the book while out in the forest, and pleasure in browsing through it at home, we will have succeeded.

Maggie Stuckey
George Palmer

How to
Use This Book

First off, thumb through and see what is here. There are two sections. The first is mostly words—words about trees in general. The second section, much the larger, is pictures and words—sketches of the significant Western trees, and verbal descriptions of each.

More than likely, you'll be using the book as a way to learn what tree is which while out in the forest. A few things to keep in mind as you start which will make things a bit easier:

First, which trees are covered in this book? The major woody plants native to the West and the Northwest that (1) assume a tree form (those which are usually thought of as shrubs are not included), and that (2) you'd have some chance of encountering on an average outing (rare or very sparse species are not included).

Then, standing by a tree, trying to find out its name, where do you start? With most tree books, you must work your way through the traditional dichotomous key, which most nonscientists, including us, find intimidating. Or you must study every page till you find your tree. Or you must turn to the index—which doesn't help much if you don't know the name!

We deliberately avoided the standard approaches, and developed a method which we believe is easiest to use. If you have browsed through the book, you may have noticed the small leaf drawings in the upper right-hand corner. When you are near the tree you want to identify, simply fan through the pages and stop at the one which looks like those on your tree. Use the text material and left-hand page illustrations to check for the fine details.

Maybe you are a short distance away. You can begin your identification by thumbing through the right-hand page silhouettes. Here's how: Hold the book at arm's length (so that the type is out of focus to your eyes) and stand facing the tree. A faint silhouette is printed under the words on the right-hand page. Look at both the tree and silhouette while you flip pages; soon you'll find it.

Use the silhouette also to gauge the full mature size of a tree when you're examining a young sapling. Bear in mind that all trees of the same species do not have identical silhouettes; the one shown is our attempt to sketch an "average" shape.

There are, regrettably for all of us, a number of tree species which closely resemble others. These you will not be able to pinpoint with just the silhouette or leaf key; it will require some careful study of the differences in bark, foliage, fruit, etc. To help you with these look-alikes, we have drawn up a comparison chart of the features which distinguish one from another. They are found at the end of the following group of trees:

hemlock   fir
spruce   cedar/juniper
larch

Some Basics
The Root of the Matter

A few general concepts of botany that will make your study of this and other books easier, and will enrich your pleasure in observing the trees.

A TREE IS THE SUM OF ITS PARTS, AND MORE

If you believe in definitions, a tree is a large plant, more than 15 feet high, with a single tough, woody stem (trunk) and a well-defined crown. Shrubs, on the other hand, have several trunks growing together in a clump, and are shorter than trees. Obviously, the dividing line between shrubs and trees is fuzzy; a number of plants can be considered either large shrubs or small trees, depending on who's describing them. Vine maple is a common example of this kind of tree; in fact, if it's a logger who's doing the describing, he's apt to call the sprawling vine maple a weed—and that's when he's being polite!

All trees have a typical form, a certain look, which is composed of their basic shape, texture, size, color, etc. Most species have a characteristic outline shape which helps us to identify them; a maple has a different silhouette from a spruce, for instance. But the individual parts of the tree—leaf, flower, stem, root—also contribute to the overall appearance of the tree, and a close examination of them is sometimes needed to pin down exact identification.

Leaf. Described by way they are arranged on the stem, and by their type.

Leaf Arrangements

Opposite   Alternate   Whorled

Leaf Types

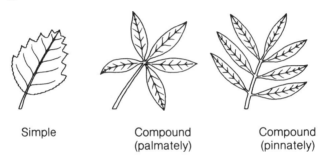

Simple   Compound   Compound
               (palmately)   (pinnately)

Flower. The flower contains the reproductive parts of the tree, which will ultimately produce a seed for the generation of a new plant. Every tree produces flowers of some sort, but some are so small, so unlike a typical flower, that we are unaware of them. You probably have never noticed, for example, the flower of a pine tree.

Fruit. Flowers develop into fruits, which contain the seed that will produce a new tree. It may be necessary to broaden your thinking on the term, for a "fruit" is not just crabapples and cherries, but also the red berries of dogwood, the cones of a fir, and the winged seeds of a maple.

Trunk, Bark, Twig, Roots. As an element that we consider in identifying a tree, we must look at the trunk in two ways: its shape, and the character of its bark. Likewise, the look of the small stems—be they hairy or smooth, thin or stout—is a part of a tree's general quality. As observers, we are not normally aware of root structure, but it is clearly important to the continued health of a tree, and will in some ways determine the physical qualities of the above-ground appearance.

SCIENTIFIC AND COMMON NAMES

If you feel a little lost trying to deal with long scientific names, relax—you're in good company. Perhaps it would help if you knew the reasoning behind the naming system.

The common name by which a plant is known in one part of the country may be quite different from its common name in another place; it may take quite a while before persons from two different locales realize they're not talking about the same tree, even though they call it the same name.

On the other hand, every plant now known to exist has one, and only one, scientific name. Thus a botanist in Norway can talk to a professor in Mexico, and both can be assured of the correct identity of the tree they're discussing.

As unofficial naturalists, we are going to need only the genus and species names. The genus is the "family"* group, and the species designates each separate member of the family. Maple is a genus, vine maple is a species. In print, scientific names are italicized (or underlined, if you don't have italics); the genus name is capitalized, the species name is lower case. If several of a family are discussed together, after the first name the genus is abbreviated by first letter only. For example, *Acer circinatum* and *A. macrophyllum*.

Do you have to learn the scientific names? No, you don't. But it's rather fun to know a few, and know how to pronounce them, and then amaze your friends and family on your next hike. It isn't as hard as it may first appear. Let's take a few examples.

Pseudotsuga menziesii—Douglas fir

Pseudo—means "false." You already know how to pronounce it.

tsuga—means hemlock. Because this tree somewhat resembles hemlock. Pronounced *"soo*-gah".

menziesii—named in honor of Archibald Menzies, a famous Scottish botanist of the early 19th Century. Pronounced "men-*zeez*-ee-eye."

---

*We use the term informally here. In strict scientific usage, "family" designates a group of genera which is botanically related.

Tsuga heterophylla—Western hemlock

Tsuga—now you know what that means, and how to pronounce it.

hetero—means "different" (think of heterosexual, and heterogeneous).

phylla—means "leaves." *Heterophylla,* then, means having different leaves on the same plant (a reference to the fact that needles of this tree are of different length).

Acer macrophyllum—Bigleaf maple

Acer—the Latin name for maple. Pronounced *Ace*-er.

macro—means "big." As in macrocosm.

phyllum—another form of the word for "leaf." Therefore, *macrophyllum* is "bigleaf."

DECIDUOUS AND EVERGREEN TREES

We think of trees in two primary groups: those who lose all their leaves in the same season each year, and those with leaves the year 'round. The life of the leaves of a deciduous tree has a direct relationship to the length of sunlight available in any one day. As the days get shorter in the fall, leaves of these trees produce less chlorophyll, because the production process (called photosynthesis) can take place only in the presence of sunlight. The leaves gradually lose their component of chlorophyll (which is green), and thus the less prominent yellow and red colorings become visible. We see a brief show of autumn color, and then the leaves die and fall to the ground.

Evergreen trees also lose their leaves, but it is a gradual process, and dead leaves are constantly replaced by new ones. Evergreen trees can have narrow leaves (pine needles, for example), tiny scale-like leaves (like junipers), or broad leaves (like many familiar flowering shrubs, such as rhododendrons and camellias).

How and Where A Tree Grows, and Why

A mature tree is a living example of the interaction between the hereditary characteristics of an organism, and the environment in which it grows. Though the tiny seed of a redwood contains all the genetic information to make a giant tree, if it does not find a favorable environment, it will not grow at all.

Environmental forces which affect trees (and all plants, for that matter), are in two principal groups: *climate,* which is composed of temperature, precipitation, solar radiaton, and wind; and *soil* characteristics, such as texture, structure, depth, moisture-holding capacity, drainage rate, nutrient content, and topographic position. Elevation and latitude also influence trees. There are also biological forces which influence plant growth: plant associates, larger animals that use trees as a source of food and shelter, small animals, insects, fungi, and a myriad of microorganisms.

The next time you look at a tree (or even a house plant) give a moment of thought to the complexity of forces which have produced the organism before you. We'd like to give you a more detailed glimpse of those forces, in hopes that your appreciation of trees and forests will be enhanced.

Moisture. Water availability is a limiting factor. If there is too little moisture, seeds will not germinate, and trees will wilt and die. Moisture begins as precipitation—snow, rain, or "fogdrip." But it is not just the total amount of precipitation that matters; the seasonal distribution is also important. If the rain doesn't come when there is growing light available, trees do not develop well.

Temperature. A crucial influence. Plants grow much faster when it is warmer; the rate of growth may double with every 18°F. But there are limits. Each plant has its own set of maximum, minimum, and optimum temperatures which govern its development. Outside this range, the plant cannot survive.

Not only do plants respond to temperature limits, but some are strongly affected by thermo-periodicity—the alternation of daily or seasonal temperatures. If the difference between the low temperature at night and the high during the day is not great enough, flowers don't flower, seeds may not be developed, new leaves may not form.

Light. Essential to photosynthesis, the process by which plants make food from carbon dioxide and water in the presence of sunlight. But the quality, intensity, and duration of light all affect the photosynthetic process. Trees vary as to the amount of light intensity at which maximum photosynthesis goes on.

The duration of light is also a powerful force. The opening of spring buds is triggered by light duration, and the fall colors of maples, oaks and other deciduous trees are triggered by length of daylight. Unequal distribution of light may affect the shape of a tree as it leans toward the light, developing more foliage on the more lighted side.

Air Movement. While it is not really important in the greater scheme of things, wind can have important local effects, by sculpting tree forms, and by accelerating the loss of water from plants and the soil.

Soil Condition. Soil is the medium in which trees are anchored, and a tree can tell you a lot about that medium. Most trees grow with straight trunks. But if the soil is not stable, it will move, thus moving the tree, which adjusts to a new upright position, causing a curved trunk. If you see a lot of trees with trunks curved the same way, you are probably standing on unstable, slowly moving ground.

Soil provides all essential elements required for growth except those obtained from the atmosphere. Soil directly affects plant growth because it controls the supply of moisture and nutrients the plant needs. When you are curious about a new tree, dig down into the soil with your hands. Get a feel for it. Did you know that soil has a smell? Good soil smells sweet and "earthy;" not-so-good soils may smell sour or rank. Is it heavy or light and fluffy; sandy or like fudge? This is the soil which produced the tree before you, and it may be up to 10 feet deep.

Topographic Position. In relative terms, location on a hillside or level plane influences not only the kind of soil in that area, but also the kind of trees that may grow in that soil. The next time you are standing on a hillside, looking south, consider that the south-facing slope gets a lot more sun than the north-facing slope behind you. Because of this, the south-facing slope is warmer and drier. On the other hand, the north-facing slope, because it lies in its own shadow, is cooler and more moist. Consequently the species of trees on the two sides of the hill may be very different. Keep in mind that cold-natured species usually indicate cold campsites.

Ravines, gulleys and narrow valleys also affect which kinds of trees grow there. Cold air flows downhill, so the bottom of a valley may have a wider range of daily high and low temperatures than a point higher on either slope; this affects the metabolic processes we spoke of earlier, and trees that have a narrow temperature tolerance range may not survive.

Elevation. Elevation is closely related to temperature. Not considering the influence of weather itself, it gets 3°F cooler for every 1000 feet higher you go. These three degrees may contribute to dramatic changes in the tree types as you gain elevation; consider the vegetation change at the timberline level.

Latitude. The farther north we go, the colder it gets. The average annual temperature is 1½ to 2 degrees cooler for every degree of latitude (which is approximately 70 miles). A tree which thrives in a warm setting, with a long summer, cannot adapt to the cooler areas farther north. Latitude and elevation work together to influence what tree grows where.

Consider, too, that the farther north you go, the cooler it is at low elevations. This means that trees which are tolerant to cold are found at lower and lower elevations as you go farther north. The illustration below will give you an idea of this effect.

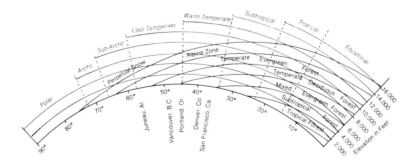

What does all this mean to you? Well, we believe that a tree is much more than a botanical name. If we know some of its habits and characteristics, we can know something about the environment that affected it; we can then conclude something about how that environment might affect us in turn. While the full study of plant habits is far too complex to present here, it is our hope that once you know the name of a tree and have some awareness of the environmental forces at work, you will want to look more closely at the trees around you, and feel a closer identity with the land which is their home, and ours.

Learning to Know A Tree

On a walk along a forest trail, while picnicking in a city park, or driving along a mountain highway, we are all touched, often awed, by the strength and beauty of the trees that share this land with us. To be curious about these magnificent plants, to want to know more about them and their role in our world, is a natural extension of the pleasure we derive from them; and so we find ourselves wondering, "What tree is that?"

If you take a minute to think about it, you will find that you already know some trees, have known them for so long you don't even remember when you learned them. And knowing these, you may want to learn others. Sometimes the learning process can seem overwhelming; it's very common, for instance, to feel that all evergreens look alike. . .to lose sight of the trees because of the forest. We who live in the Western and Northwestern states find the task even more difficult because our trees are often of such enormous size; when a tree is towering high above you, it's well nigh impossible to grasp its identity and its character.

But you can recognize in the quickest glance, the trees that you already know. You don't have to closely inspect leaf or fruit or twig, you just *know*. When this happens, you have viewed the *whole* tree, assessing its size, shape, color, density, texture and a dozen other qualities, all in an instant, and you remember the name.

But what if you don't already know what tree that is? To be absolutely certain of the exact name, there is an established ritual of identification, a ritual which asks certain specific questions and seeks certain answers. (A little later on, we're going to describe, in a general way, how that process works.) Botanists, like all scientists, use a very precise and technical vocabulary, which to laypeople seems too immense to learn. How, then, can we identify trees in the easiest way?

A satisfying shortcut is to learn key points which distinguish *families* of trees. Even though you may not know, or want to know, the exact species, you will find that you get a kick out of knowing that a particular tree is clearly a pine and not a fir. The chart below will get you started.

TO KNOW A TREE IN AN INSTANT

Significant Keys to Identification of Native Western Trees

IF YOU SEE		THE TREE IS
An acorn		An oak
A double seed with "propeller" wings		A maple
Sharp thorns on the stem		A hawthorne
Peeling bark and orange trunk		A madrone

---

IF YOU SEE		THE TREE IS
Long needles in bundles of 2 to 5		A pine
Short needles in bundles of 10 or more		A larch
Short single needles and bright red berries		A yew
Short single needles and this unique cone		A Douglas fir
Short single needles that are very stiff and pointy		A spruce
Short single needles on a tree whose top droops over		A hemlock

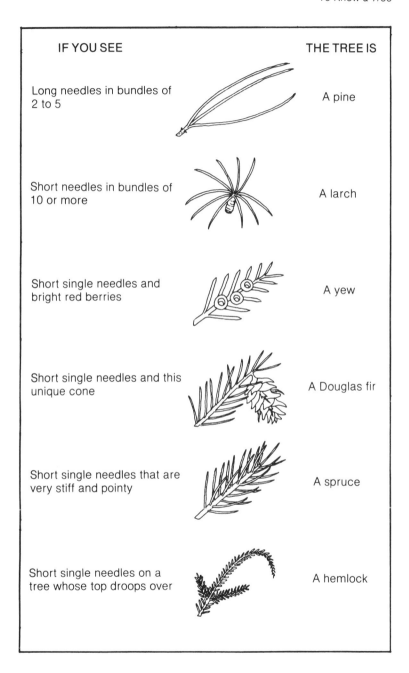

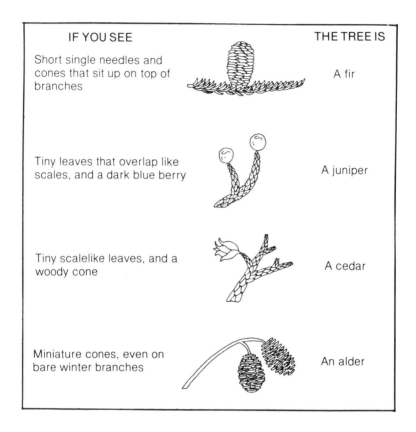

IF YOU SEE		THE TREE IS
Short single needles and cones that sit up on top of branches		A fir
Tiny leaves that overlap like scales, and a dark blue berry		A juniper
Tiny scalelike leaves, and a woody cone		A cedar
Miniature cones, even on bare winter branches		An alder

For most of our broad-leaf trees, the surest, fastest key to identity is what the leaf itself looks like; these, regrettably, we must learn individually.

Once you have pinpointed the general family of a tree, you may want to go further and identify the particular species. But how do you go about it? Where do you look first, and what do you look for? What is there about the structure of a particular tree that makes it different from another, and how is that difference described?

Speaking generally, the process involves examining the parts of a tree individually, in close enough detail to isolate a point of difference. Using this book or any other reference, you will quickly come to know the aspects of tree structure that have a bearing on tree identification, and learn how to evaluate the descriptive text. Let's say you see in the field a tree you're curious about. You look through your book on trees until you find an illustration that looks the same, and you read that this species has alternate branching. You look closely at this aspect of your tree; if you see opposite branching, you know you're on the wrong page. If your tree has alternate branching, you *may* have found the correct reference. . .but you move on, and check out the next point.

What are the primary points to look for?

Start with the Leaves

Your first step is almost always the *foliage*. That is, what do the leaves look like? This will tell you if you're looking at a needle-leaf or scale-leaf evergreen, a broad-leaf evergreen, or a broad-leaf deciduous tree. If the tree you are curious about is so tall that you can't pick off a leaf, look on the ground immediately below for fallen leaves or branches. Remember, too, that young trees in the immediate area were most likely started by seeds from the big tree.

In the winter, you can easily tell deciduous trees from all others: they're the one without leaves. To identify a deciduous tree in the winter is a bit tricky; look on the tree for persistent dead leaves or fruits; look on the ground for dead leaves; for die-hard detectives, there's a sophisticated system based on buds. In all other seasons, you'll examine leaf shape, flower and fruit to distinguish among species.

Identifying Needle-Leaf Evergreens

If the tree is a needle-leaf evergreen, the next place to look is the *arrangement of the needles*. For example, if there are long needles in bundles of 2 to 5, it's a pine, simple as that. But if you see short needles attached individually along the twig, your tree may be a fir, a Douglas fir, a spruce, a hemlock, a yew, or a redwood. We don't find the answer from foliage alone, so we must look for other clues. For the next step, turn to the cone.

Cones are the fruits of evergreen conifer trees, and the second clue to identify. When you examine a cone this way, you will need to make note of:

- size
- color
- shape
- position on branch: does it sit upright, hang down or curve backward?
- size and shape of bracts, if any
- shape and arrangement of cone scales
- how and when they lose their scales

27

Bark is the next logical place to look for identity clues. Some of the qualities used to distinguish different barks are:

- color
- texture: is it smooth or rough?
- thickness: is it thin or thick?
- physical makeup: does the bark form big flakes, long strips, small squares? Does it have any deep grooves, and which direction do they run?

And so we continue through the tree, looking more and more closely until we find a point of absolute difference. Sometimes the differences are slight: in this book we have four pines which have 5 needles in a bundle. You will also find that firs are very difficult to tell apart. It then becomes necessary to carefully examine the small differences between cones and foliage.

Identifying Scale-Leaf Evergreens

Scale-leaf evergreens are those which have very small leaves, set tightly along the stem and overlapping each other like fish scales. Here in the West we have only four native scale-leaf trees, all members of the Cypress family. Because the leaves are so small, we are not aware of them as individuals, and find it hard to assign a particular character to them. To tell the difference between the four types of trees, we start with fruit. And immediately we see that there are two basic types: a dark blue berry, and a woody cone. The blue berries are found on junipers, and the cones on one of several trees commonly called cedars. Two species have cones that are quite similar, and so we then take a close look at the foliage. (For a detailed look at this family of trees, see page 131. Here we are only talking of the process in general terms.)

Identifying Broad-Leaf Trees

Look first at the *leaves.* You will need to observe the following:

- size: length and width
- color, both on top and on the underside; seasonal color change
- texture: is it thick and leathery, thin, rough, smooth, etc.?
- physical nature: is it a simple leaf (all in one unit), or compound (made of several leaflets)?
- shape: for instance, oval or round; if leaf has lobes, how many, and what is their nature?
- position relative to other leaves: alternate or opposite?
- do the margins (edges) have tiny teeth, or are they smooth?

Branching habit will often provide a clue.

- Are branches and twigs opposite or alternate?
- Do branches grow upward (ascending), turn downward (descending), or stick straight out (horizontal)?

The *bark* should next be examined, using the same questions as those outlined for needle-leaf trees above.

Flowers, in their season, provide a particularly dramatic set of identifying characteristics. Make note of:

- color
- size
- shape
- physical arrangement: are they individual blossoms, in a cluster, in a long catkin, etc.?
- position on branch

Fruit, when it is present, is also a memorable way to tell the difference between trees. Look for:

- size
- color
- shape
- position on branch

Another significant way we know one tree from another is by the geographic area it grows in, and what trees normally grow alongside it. If you know, for example, that a certain tree grows only in the coastal fog zone, you'll know not to expect to see it high on the mountain.

And another major element is the overall shape and form of the tree. This is something you can learn from a book only in a very general way, and then refine and solidify your understanding by looking at lots of trees. Then you will get to know your tree by its size and shape: you will know that that tree at the edge of the field is not a dogwood because a dogwood doesn't get that big, and doesn't have that heavy, rounded look to it.

Finally, after you have poked around and smelled, touched, and looked at enough trees, someday you will realize that you know which tree it is just because of its nature, or spirit, or personality; you have absorbed what a friend refers to as the *gestalt* of the tree, and it is forever yours.

Glossary

Scientific Vocabulary for Ordinary People

As editors, we want this book to be useful and handy to just about everyone. One of our goals is to make sure that people without scientific training can use and enjoy the book, and so we have tried to present the material in everyday English.

But there are some terms for which there is simply no everyday substitute. It's a little like trying to talk about a zipper without saying the word "zipper." You could do it, but you'd end up using a lot of extra words, and you'd still run the risk of not being absolutely clear.

Sometimes, there's no way around using a technical term. We have included here a list of those words used in this book which may be new to you. You'll find that by the time you have referred to this glossary once or twice, you have learned the word and incorporated it into your own vocabulary. We think you'll find it fun to know these terms, and that this knowledge will become one small way to further enrich your enjoyment of the outdoors.

USEFUL WORDS TO KNOW

Abundant   Plentiful. Large numbers of a species are present in one area. Abundant has a geographic overtone—as in locally or regionally abundant. See also *Widespread*.

Alpine,
Alpine Zone   Refers to a specific combination of environmental conditions. The "alpine" is the highest, coldest, most severe climate in the area. It is linked to elevation, but the exact elevation varies with latitude. (See chart on page 21.) That is, the alpine zone in southern Oregon may be at an elevation much higher than the alpine zone in Alaska. Basically, the alpine zone is the one in which no erect tree forms grow; the "trees" have a stunted and gnarled form. See also *Timberline*.

Alternate   Refers to a type of plant structure in which new leaves and twigs appear on alternating sides of the stem. See also *Opposite*.

Bloom   A waxy substance, usually white or gray, which covers either foliage or fruit, or both. It can be rubbed off.

Bract   A modified leaf. We are likely to see two kinds: the thin "interleaves" between the scales on a cone, sometimes sticking out beyond them; and the structures found just below the base of some flowers, and sometimes mistaken for the flowers themselves. The white or pink "petals" of the dogwood flowers, for instance, are really bracts.

Catkin   A long, thin, dense cluster of male or female flowers, attached to a common, usually drooping, stem. A pussy willow is a short, fat catkin. Often dried catkins remain on a tree long after flowering.

Compound   Refers to a type of leaf structure. Compound leaves are composed of

31

several leaflets on a common stalk. See also *Simple.*

Compound leaf

Crown The word has several meanings in the botanical world. In this book, "crown" refers to the area of a tree from which leaf-bearing branches grow.

Conifer A tree which bears cones as its fruit. Usually, conifers are evergreen, and sometimes the terms are used interchangeably, but this is misleading, as a few conifers (such as larch) are *not* evergreen.

Deciduous (dee-*sid*-you-us) Trees which lose all their leaves each year, often preceded by a glorious display of autumn color. Term is used in two ways: we speak of a "deciduous tree," as contrasted to evergreen; and we describe a winter tree, devoid of leaves, as being "in its deciduous state." See also *Evergreen.*

Dominant The species which, by virtue of its number, coverage, or size, exerts considerable influence upon the other species sharing the same space. The dominant species often determines the "look" or overall appearance of a particular forest area.

Evergreen Trees which do not lose all their leaves each winter. The term does not mean "permanent;" evergreen leaves do fall after several years of life, but there are always newer leaves present, so that the tree is never without leaves. See also *Deciduous.*

Fruit The part of a tree that contains the

seed from which a new tree may grow. A pine cone is thus as much a "fruit" as a cherry.

Genus A term used in the system of plant classification and naming, which refers to a group of closely related species. All oaks make up one genus, all pines another genus, and so on. The *generic* name of a plant is always written in italics, and always capitalized. (If you don't have italics, then the genus and species names should be underlined.) See also *Species*.

Leader The topmost part of the central, main stem of a tree, above the highest branches. The part of the tree that is actively growing taller.

Leaf The green structure of a tree, which contains the chlorophyll that makes possible the manufacture of food. The needles of a pine tree are its leaves, and the small scales of a juniper are its leaves.

Lenticel A short horizontal mark in the bark of some trees, particularly noticeable in cherries. Lenticels are areas of loosely arranged porous cells through which gases may pass.

Margin The edge of a leaf.

Native As it relates to plants, the term means those which naturally grow in a certain locale, and grow there without any influence from man, either past or present.

Opposite Describes a type of structure in which leaves and twigs grow in pairs, on opposite sides of the stem. See also *Alternate*.

Pendent   Hanging downward from the branch; in this book usually used in reference to the position of cones.

Petiole   The "stem" which attaches leaf to branch.

Pyramidal   A term used to describe the tree shape that is broad at the base, and pointed at the top, with more or less symmetrical sides. . . shaped, that is, like a pyramid.

Scalelike   This is a specific term, describing the shape and arrangement of leaves that are very short, set closely on the stem, and overlap each other like scales on a fish. Junipers and cedars have scalelike leaves.

Simple   The entire leaf is one complete surface, not divided into leaflets. Contrasted to *Compound*, which see.

Species   The basic name in plant classification, with the most specific descriptors. Western hemlock and mountain hemlock are two separate *species* of the same *genus*. The species is always used in conjunction with a genus name, should always be italicized or underlined, and begins with a lower-case letter. When two or more species of the same genus are referred to together, often the second and succeeding names are abbreviated, like this: *Tsuga heterophylla* and *T. mertensiana*. Plants in the same species interbreed freely, making possible the huge array of commercial landscaping plants. Plants of different species do not—usually—interbreed.

Stand
: A grove of trees. Stands may be "mixed," with several species present, or "pure," with only one species growing.

Stem
: The stiff part of a plant, through which water and nutrients are carried from the roots to the leaves. Thus a stem is anything from a trunk (which is the "main stem" of a tree), to a branch, to the smallest twig.

Subalpine
: The climate zone just below alpine; cold and harsh, but where some erect trees are found.

Sucker
: A new-growth stem which arises from the base of a trunk or from the roots. For some plants, suckering is a regeneration technique; a tree which has been cut or burned, but whose roots are still healthy, will produce suckers to replace the old tree.

Terminal
: At the outermost end of a branch or twig, as in "terminal bud."

Timberline
: Demarks the lower edge of the alpine zone, and therefore the line above which erect trees will not grow.

Twig
: See *Stem*.

Two-ranked
: Describes a particular way leaves or flowers are set on a branch: in two distinct rows, opposite to each other but in the same plane. (See the foliage of grand fir, page 111.) Contrasted to those leaves which are arranged all around the twig, or those which are attached to just one side.

Understory   The lower strata of plants growing underneath the largest trees in any particular forest: shrubs, flowers, ferns, grasses, etc. Small or even medium-sized trees can be understory plants, if they are growing beneath larger trees.

Whorl   The name for a particular kind of leaf or stem arrangement. When more than two leaves or branches originate from the same point on the stem, they are arranged in a "whorl." In contrast to *Alternate* or *Opposite* arrangements (see each).

Widespread   Occurring over a broad geographic range. See also *Abundant*. A tree species can be locally abundant without being widespread, and vice versa. If the tree is found only in a certain part of western Colorado, it is not *widespread;* if, however, there are many thick stands in that location, this tree is *abundant* there. If a tree grows in 39 of the 48 continental states, it is *widespread;* if there are only a few trees growing together at any one spot, it is not *abundant.*

Windthrow   The phenomenon of live trees being blown down from their location by severe winds. Tree which are subject to windthrow damage are often those with shallow root systems. Trees which can withstand heavy winds are said to be "windfirm."

Tree Finder for the Western Area

☐ —No Trees. Desert or Prairie.

☐ —Clumps of Trees. High Desert or Prairie Edge.

■ —Forest.

■ —No Trees. Alpine Zone.

BIGLEAF MAPLE
Acer macrophyllum
Ace-er mack-ro-*fill*-um

Key Identifier. Unbelievably huge leaves—up to 12 inches long, or more.

General Shape. Form of the tree varies greatly, depending on the soil, moisture conditions, competition from other trees, etc. Forest-grown trees may reach 60 to 80 feet with a 30 inch diameter. In the open, bigleaf maple is often a short tree 20 to 30 feet high, with a crooked trunk.

Leaves. Simple, opposite leaves are separated into 5 lobes, each with a deep, broad, rounded cleft. Margins are smooth (in contrast to many maples) but they have several very large blunt-tip notches. Leaves are dark green and shiny above, paler below; in autumn they turn a dull yellow before falling. It is their immense size, 6 to 12 inches (the largest of any maple), which makes them immediately recognizable. Leaf petioles "bleed" a milky fluid when cut or squeezed.

Flowers. Long clusters of scented yellow blossoms appear in spring, as the new leaves begin to grow.

Fruit. Fruit is a pair of seeds, thickly covered with fuzzy brown hairs, with 2 (or sometimes 3 or 4) wings, in an upside-down V shape, each 1½ to 2 inches long. Fruits mature in fall and when they fall they twirl like helicopters.

Bark, Twigs. Bark is smooth and gray-brown at first, then becomes red-brown and ridged on older trees. Twigs are thick and smooth, green to dark red; the terminal bud is blunt and dark red.

The bigleaf (or "Oregon") is the only large maple tree that is native to the West; there is no way to confuse it with other maples in this area. It is normally found along year-round streams or in the moist hollows of north- or east-facing slopes. It thrives where summers are relatively cool, but winters relatively mild, and where there is a heavy amount of precipitation, especially in winter. . .a good description of the Pacific Northwest states, west of the Cascades. Bigleaf maple inhabits the lower elevations, and is usually found growing individually or in small clusters with other trees, rather than in large stands.

The natives of the Northwest states found it a most useful resource. The bark was made into rope; the leaves were used as "lids" in cooking and as work surfaces for preparing food; the wood made excellent fires for smoking meat and fish. The wood of these trees was the basic material for carving wooden implements and decorations; it was also used for canoe paddles, and it was the basic construction timber.

The seeds are food source for mice, woodrats, squirrels, chipmunks, and some birds. Young saplings, with their tender leaves and twigs, are an important browse food for black-tailed and mule deer. The tree sprouts very easily from the stump when cut.

The wood of bigleaf maple could be used for furniture and other fine woodworking, but because it doesn't form large pure stands, it's considered difficult to harvest and therefore is little used commercially.

Key Identifier. Leaf shape—like a perfect circle with notches.

General Shape. Varies from a small tree to large shrub. Very often the tree has several trunks, and frequently one or more of the trunks sprawl along the ground, like a vine. Commonly 15 to 20 feet high, occasionally up to 40 feet. The foliage is usually sparse, giving the tree an open, airy appearance.

Leaves. Simple, opposite leaves are almost circular in outline shape; that is, if you draw a line connecting all the tips, it would make an almost perfect circle. They are 2 to 6 inches in diameter, with either 7 or 9 lobes; each lobe has small teeth on the sides and a sharp point at the tip. Leaves are dark green above, paler below, with small tufts of hair on the underside. In the fall, leaves turn brilliant red, yellow and orange.

Flowers. Small clusters of purple and white flowers are not especially showy.

Fruit. A pair of seeds (occasionally 3 or 4), each with a reddish-brown wing about ¾ inch long; the wings are spread very widely.

Bark. Bark is thin, smooth, gray-brown or red-brown; on older trees, bark becomes vaguely furrowed.

Vine maple (sometimes called mountain maple) is a very common understory tree in the Northwest; it has the same moisture needs as the Douglas fir, and so is usually found scattered among the large firs of this area. Vine maple quickly takes hold in logged-over areas, abandoned roads, and recent landslide scars, and so is an important first step in the regreening of these areas.

Vine maple gives us one of the most brilliant fall color shows, with bright reds and yellows mixed together, even on the same leaf. But even this visual treat does not endear the tree to loggers and lumbermen, who have struggled for years against its whiplike stems, which sometimes seem expressly designed for tripping humans.

The Quinault Indians of Washington state called this the "basket tree," for they found that the young shoots in spring were excellent material for weaving. Slender stems were used to construct fish traps. The green branches burn very poorly and so were used by woodsmen for pot hangers, reflectors, and cooking sticks.

BITTER CHERRY
Prunus emarginata
Prune-us ee-margin-*ate*-ah

Key Identifier. Leaf, bark, flower and fruit are typical of all cherry trees (see below); bitter cherry has flowers and fruit in small, rounded clusters. See chart on page 45 for species comparisons.

General Form. Usually bitter cherry is a small shrubby tree, with multiple trunks forming a dense thicket. On good open sites, it becomes a smallish tree, with a straight, slender trunk and a short crown of ascending branches.

Leaves. Most members of the *Prunus* genus have similar leaves: simple, alternate, more or less oval-shaped, and usually with small teeth on the margins. Leaves of bitter cherry are roughly 1 to 3 inches long and ½ to 1½ inches wide, although leaves of different sizes are frequently found on the same branch. They are dark green above, paler below; leaves or stems variably to very hairy. There are two small glands on the leaf near the base.

Flowers. White blossoms are about ½ inch wide, and are in bundles of 6 to 12. They bloom in the spring, when the leaves are about half-mature.

Fruit. Bright red (and sometimes black) cherries are about ½ inch in diameter; they will be in small bundles, as were the flowers. The seed inside the very bitter flesh of the fruit is egg-shaped and has grooved sides.

Bark, Twigs. Like all cherry trees, this bark is thin, smooth, and marked with horizontal slits (lenticels). In bitter cherry, the bark is brown, with short bright orange lenticels. It has a very bitter quinine taste. The bark can be easily peeled from the trunk. Twigs are shiny brown.

Bitter cherry is a small tree which brings a brilliant flower show to the forest in spring. By and large this species grows in moist areas, and in open, sunny locations; it does not tolerate shade. It is commonly found on hillslopes and along stream banks, in the form of shrubby thickets. In open situations, bitter cherry can become a modest-sized tree, 40 to 50 feet high and 6 to 12 inches thick. The largest known living tree is 62 feet high and 56 feet wide, with a trunk that is 2 feet 11 inches thick.

While humans consider the bitter cherry fruit inedible, many forest songbirds, including the cedar waxwing, relish these treats. The seed pits are not broken down in digestion, and therefore are scattered by the birds all over their area.

Northwest Indians found many uses for the bark of this tree. When polished to a rich color, it made a shiny dark "ribbon" for interweaving into baskets and other utensils. Women were given pieces of the bark to chew during childbirth, in the belief it would ease their discomfort. The bark was also brewed into a tea for use as a laxative or cold medicine, and decayed wood, when mixed with water and drunk, was thought to have contraceptive properties.

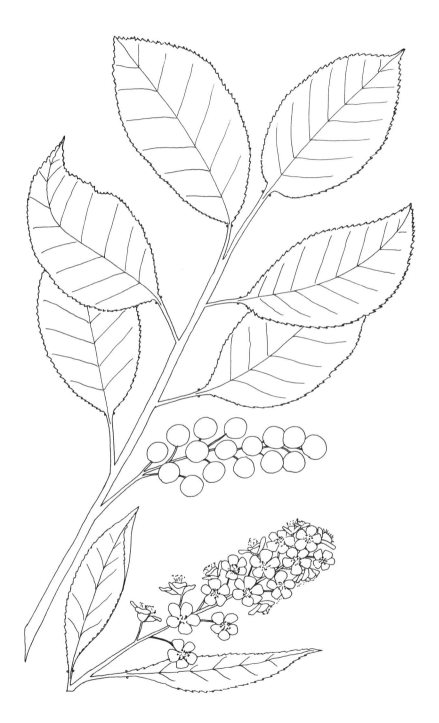

44

CHOKECHERRY
Prunus virginiana
Prune-us vir-*gin*-ee-*an*-ah

Key Identifier. All the general characteristics of cherry trees. Flowers and fruit in long clusters, like grapes. See below for species comparisons.

General Shape. A small tree or a shrub, 10 to 25 feet high and 4 to 6 inches thick. Trunks are slender and often crooked; the crown is narrow and branches are slender and horizontally spreading.

Leaves. Leaves are alternate, simple, and have fine teeth on the edges. They are 2 to 4 inches long and 1 to 2 inches wide. Top half of the leaf is wider than lower half, and narrows quickly to a sharp point. Dark green above; bottom is lighter green and may be covered with tiny soft hairs. There are two bumps, the size of pin heads, on the stem near the base of the leaf.

Flowers. White blossoms are ½ inch wide, and grouped into long clusters 3 to 6 inches long; clusters may have as many as 20 flowers.

Fruit. Red cherries, sometimes reddish-black, are grouped together in a long, drooping cluster, rather like grapes. Cherries are about ¼ inch in diameter and, although sour, are quite edible.

Bark, Twigs. Bark is thin, smooth, and marked with horizontal lenticels (the bark of all cherry trees is similar); color is gray- or red-brown. On very old trees, the bark becomes less smooth and more scaly. It is difficult to peel. New twigs are downy, with a sharp-pointed terminal bud.

The chokecherry is found throughout most of the continental U.S., usually on lower mountain slopes and beside streams; however, it does not extend to the very humid forests along the Pacific Coast. In the Northwest, it is more common on the eastern side of the Cascade crest. Like many uncultivated cherries, this is a small tree, often more like a shrub; the largest one known, in Michigan, is 66 feet high and 56 feet wide. The cherries of this tree are a great treat to songbirds; also to people, when baked into a pie. The fruit was eaten by many Indian tribes, and pounded with meat into pemmican. It is recorded that Sacajawea was captured by an enemy tribe while she was in a chokecherry thicket, enjoying the fruit, and taken west to the Dakotas, where Lewis and Clark later met her and convinced her to serve their expedition as guide. Among the Navajo tribes, chokecherry is considered sacred.

TO DISTINGUISH BETWEEN WILD CHERRIES

Chokecherry Up to 20 flowers and fruit in long clusters. Mature bark is scaly and hard to peel; lenticels disappear with age. Leaves have two small nodules on the petiole near the base of the leaf.

Bitter cherry Flowers and fruit in small bunches of 6 or so. Bark is smooth and peels easily; lenticels always present. Very tiny nodules are on the leaf itself, near the base.

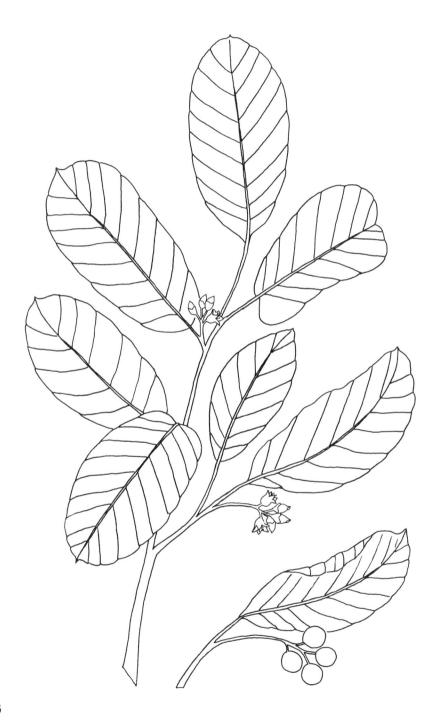

CASCARA BUCKTHORN
Rhamnus purshiana
Ram-nus *persh*-ee-*an*na

Key Identifier. Open bud, not covered with tight scales. Intensely bitter bark. Cascara is sometimes confused with young alders; remember that alders carry the very distinctive miniature cones.

General Shape. Form varies in different climates and locales. In rich, moist soils, forest-grown trees are 20 to 30 feet high, with a straight trunk and a narrow open crown; when grown in the open, trunk is shorter and branches much larger. In drier climates in the southern part of its range, cascara is usually a shrub, about 6 feet high, with several slender stems together in a clump.

Leaves. Alternate, simple leaf is oblong in shape, with a slight point. Color is light green above; underneath it is lighter color and covered with sparse hairs along veins. Margins may have small teeth, and the veins are very prominent. Leaves turn yellow in autumn.

Flowers. Very small, green, altogether insignificant.

Fruit. Fruit is fleshy, like a cherry, ¼ to ½ inch in diameter, and sweet; it is red at first, then turns a blue-black color. Each berry contains either 2 or 3 seeds.

Bark, Twigs. Bark is thin, gray or brown, and either smooth or broken into small scales. It sometimes resembles the bark of alders. Twigs are an unusual feature of the tree: cascara does not have a terminal bud in the usual sense, but side buds along the twig, at the point where the last year's leaves joined the stem. These buds are not encased with tight, overlapping protective scales, as are most trees; the budding leaves are distinctly visible, covered only with brown hairs.

The cascara is an understory tree, which grows in moist locations in the shade of larger trees. Its berries provide food to birds, raccoons, and grouse, who help to spread the seeds, but otherwise its primary significance is its bark.

The bark of the cascara (the word itself means "bark" in Spanish) has very important medicinal qualities, and it is the key ingredient in several laxative and general tonic formulas. So common is this use of the bark that it has given rise to a specialized industry: the Pacific Northwest produces all of the world's supply of cascara drug, and many local and itinerant workers are employed to harvest the bark by peeling it from the tree. The development of synthetics in recent years has somewhat reduced the demand for the bark, but as recently as 15 or 20 years ago, 5 million pounds of bark were collected every year.

Since peeling the bark kills the tree, it is seldom that we see a tree more than 30 feet high or 6 inches thick; a 6-inch diameter tree will produce about 30 pounds of bark and so is certain to be stripped by the time it reaches that size.

A modern conservation program has been built around the ability of the tree to sprout very quickly from a "live" stump, if the stump still has healthy bark. To preserve a stump that is able to sprout, bark peelers are now encouraged to cut down the tree first before peeling.

48

BLACK HAWTHORN
Crataegus douglasii
Crah-*tay*-gus *doug*las-eye

Key Identifier. Strong, needle-sharp thorns.

General Shape. This is usually a low, wide-spreading bushy tree, often growing in thickets. Occasionally, in very open locations, it may be 20 to 30 feet high with a slender trunk 10 to 30 inches in diameter and a round, dense, wide-spreading crown.

Leaves. Simple, alternate leaves are somewhat oval in shape and 1 to 2 inches long and ½ to 1½ inches wide. Leaf margins are toothed, more heavily so toward the tip, and sometimes have shallow lobes. They are deep green above, slightly lighter color below.

Flowers. Small white flowers, ½ inch wide, greatly resembling apple blossoms, in broad clusters.

Fruit. Shiny black, round fruits are shaped like blueberries, and about ½ inch in diameter. Each fruit contains 5 seeds in the center of the sweet-tasting, edible flesh.

Bark, Twigs. All along the stems are stiff, sharp thorns, ½ to 1 inch long. . .an immediate clue to hawthorn identity. Twigs are bright red and have a noticeable zigzag shape. At first, bark is thin, smooth, and greenish-brown; as the tree becomes older, bark breaks into thin, scaly plates. Root system is very widespreading and firm, and the trees provide a good soil stabilizer.

The hawthorn family is one of the largest plant families known to-day. There are nearly 100 species in Europe and Asia, and more than 100 others are native to North America. To make identification even more complex, they have the dismaying habit of interbreeding and producing new strains. Fortunately for us, there are only a few species found in the Western states, and only one is widespread enough that we are likely to encounter it.

The delicate black hawthorn grows most commonly in moist areas with rich soils, although it will occasionally move into the more arid lands. Along stream banks the tree forms natural hedgerows, and with its strong root system, plays an important role as a natural erosion control. The black hawthorn can be either a shrub or a small tree; the largest known tree is only 40 feet high.

The fruit of the tree is not so popular with forest wildlife as we might imagine, but is enjoyed by some songbirds, who help to disseminate seeds.

Hawthorn wood is heavy and quite hard, but not commercially important. Sometimes local farmers use it for turning into handles for implements.

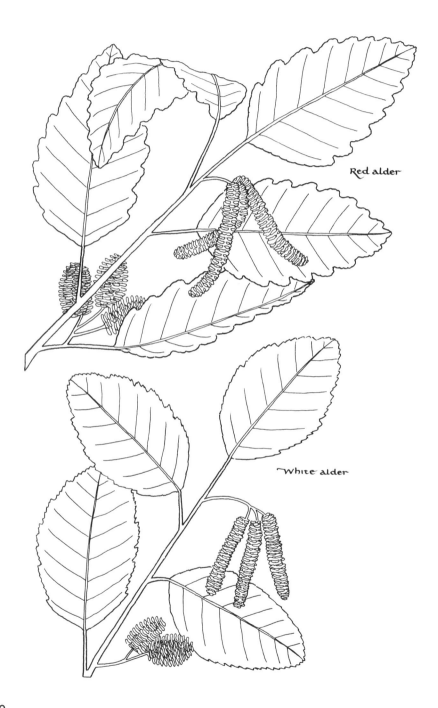

Red alder

White alder

50

RED ALDER
Alnus rubra
All-nus *rube*-rah

Key Identifier. For all alders, the tiny cone. For this species, red wood and distinctive leaves with large, blunt teeth and curled-under margins.

General Shape. Either a fair-sized shrub, 8 to 12 feet high, in a thicket along a stream; or a medium-sized slender tree, 35 to 40 feet, with abundant leaves but an overall airy look. Trunks often slightly curved.

Leaves. Alternate, simple, oval-shaped; 3 to 6 inches long and 2 to 3 inches wide. Margin has large, blunt teeth, and curls under slightly. Dull dark green above, paler underneath, often with rusty brown hairs.

Flowers. Flowers of both sexes grow on the same branch, with the male (a long catkin) usually located just over a female bud. Appear before leaves.

Fruit. A small woody cone, ½ to 1 inch long, in an oval shape that resembles a tiny Japanese lantern. Cones remain on the tree long after they lose their seeds, and so even in winter provide an instant identifier. Seeds are tiny, with very poorly developed wings, and most crash to the ground.

Bark. A ghostly greenish white, with dark blotches. Inner bark is brick red.

Like all alders, the red species grows where there is water—in the moist soil along stream banks, in areas of 25 to 120 inches of rainfall. Except along some northern Idaho streams, red alder seldom grows more than 100 miles inland from the Pacific, and usually at elevations of no more than 2500 feet. Alders are extremely fast growers (in fact, lumbermen consider them weeds), and not very long-lived; their maximum age is thought to be 100 years. They suffer few diseases; and are not often damaged by fire because they grow on damp sites with little flammable debris on the ground. Alders are intolerant of shade, and must maintain a dominant position (taller than all companions) in order to survive. Fresh avalanche sites, with access to lots of sunlight, often fill quickly with alders. Alders as a group make a significant contribution to forest ecology (see "Special Role", page 53). In addition, red alder inhibits the growth of a soil fungus that would cause heart rot in Douglas fir if it were present.

Red alder was one of the trees most widely used in woodworking by the Northwest Coast Indians. It was considered too soft for canoe paddles, but excellent for dishes and other implements, and baby cradles. The long, slow fires for smoking salmon were created with alder logs.

Alnus rhombifolia   (*all*-nus rom-bi-*foal*-ee-oh)   WHITE ALDER

Key Identifier. Inner bark stays white when peeled.

General Shape. A medium-sized tree, 50 to 80 feet high, often has multiple trunks (red alder does not) which lean enough to look unstable.

Leaves. Much like red alder, except that margin is wavy and teeth are much smaller and sharp. Leaves smaller than red alder.

Flowers. Very similar to red alder, except that they appear in midwinter.

Fruit. The typical alder cone, but slightly longer than red alder's.

Bark. On older trees, becomes red-brown and furrowed, with large plates.

White alder (in striped areas on the map above) bears many similarities to red alder, and so they are combined here. Unlike the red variety, white alder is an inland species.

51

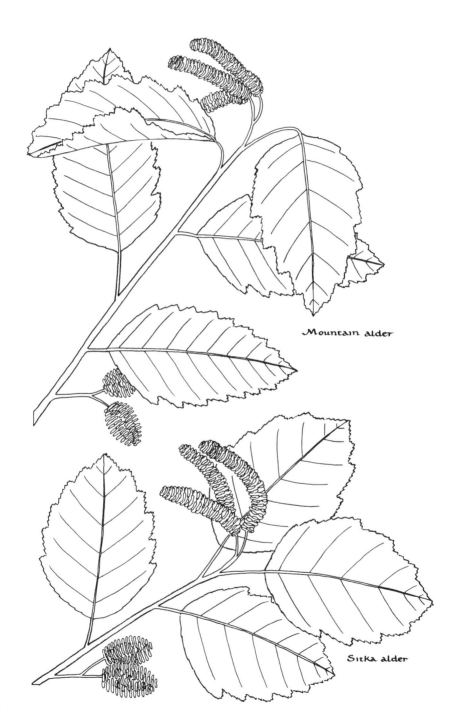

Mountain alder

Sitka alder

52

MOUNTAIN ALDER
Alnus incana
All-nus in-*can*-ah

Key Identifier. Very jagged leaf margins, with large coarse teeth which themselves have smaller teeth. Tiny cones mark it as an alder.

General Shape. A small tree or large shrub, with multiple trunks. Up to 25 feet high, with stems 6 inches thick. Often forms thickets along streams.

Leaves. Alternate, simple, oval to oblong shaped, 2 to 4 inches long. The margin is quite ragged and doubly toothed—the teeth have teeth. Dull dark green above, yellow-green and hairy below. Veins connect from midrib to tip of larger teeth; leaf tip is a broad-angled point.

Flower. Typical alder catkins, with both sexes on same twig; wind-pollinated.

Fruit. Typical alder cones, except that they fall when they are mature; seeds have two poorly developed, ineffective wings.

Bark. Younger bark is smooth, thin and dark gray-brown. Old trees develop some shallow seams and thin scales, especially near the base of the trunk.

In keeping with its name, mountain alder is usually found in the high mountain areas, 4000 feet and above; its range is shown in stripes on the map. Water-loving like all alders, this tree (also called thinleaf alder) will be found around the edges of mountain lakes, on wet, well-drained and usually rocky soils, and along stream banks. Occasionally it will follow the stream down to lower elevations. This alder does not fare well in competition with other trees, and so is usually seen in pure clumps or stands.

Alnus sinuata (*all*-nus sin-you-*ah*-tah) SITKA ALDER

Key Identifier. New leaves are sticky when young. Yellow-green and very shiny (in contrast to mountain alder) on top, paler below.

Flowers, Fruit. Much like mountain alder, except that seeds have a pair of wide, gauzy wings.

Bark. Thin, smooth, light gray with a bluish tinge.

General Shape. Almost always a medium-sized shrub, with multiple trunks. Along the coast it occasionally assumes a small tree form.

Sitka alder and mountain alder, both shrubby species, are similar in many respects, and so have been grouped together. Sitka is the most cold-resistant of all alders, and frequently grows in subalpine zones. Found in the range shown in gray above, it most often appears near water.

THE SPECIAL ROLE OF ALDERS

All the species of alder share a trait that is extremely important to the ecology of a healthy forest: the ability to fix nitrogen from the atmosphere into the soil. Nitrogen is one of the three essential nutrients for plant growth, and it must be replenished if the soil is to sustain life. Alders and some other plants (those whose fruit is a bean) contain a bacteria in their roots which combine nitrogen with oxygen from the air and make it available in the soil for plant use. Alders do even more for the soil: leaves have a high nitrogen content, and the decayed leaf litter improves the soil. Alders grow fast and are very abundant, filling in cleared, burned or avalanched areas and enriching the soil for the next cycle of growth.

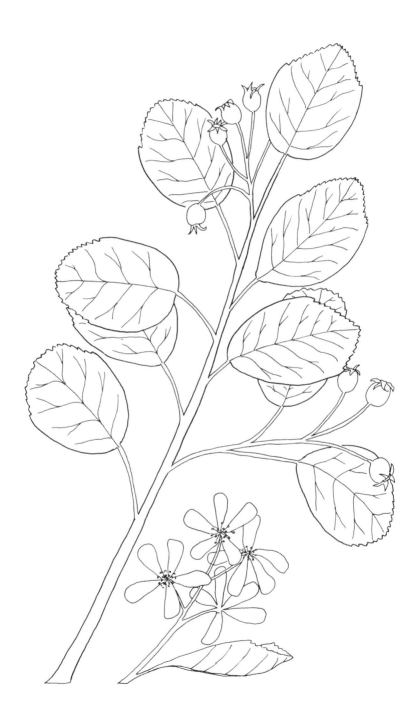

SERVICEBERRY
Amelanchier alnifolia
Am-ee-*lan*-key-er All-nee-*foal*-ee-ah

Key Identifier. Roundish leaf with teeth at end. Clusters of fragrant blossoms in spring; red or black seedy berries.

General Shape. Form is variable, depending on growing conditions. If left undisturbed, serviceberry becomes a shrubby plant, up to 12 feet high, with multiple stems and upright limbs fanning outward toward the top. More often, though, it is damaged by animals feeding on the berries, and is dwarfed to 2 feet.

Leaves. Alternate, simple, toothed leaves are ¾ to 2 inches long, more round than elliptical. The end of the leaf is squarish and notched. Young leaves are somewhat hairy below, becoming smooth as they mature.

Flowers. Small white flowers are like apple blossoms in appearance and fragrance (the serviceberry is related to the apple), and they are abundant in April and May.

Fruit. A red or black berry, about ¼ inch, contains 10 seeds.

The serviceberry is one member of a very large family of trees/shrubs that are greatly similar to each other. These plants are adapted to a wide range of conditions: both wet and dry climates, in low or medium elevations, in areas that are shady or brightly lighted.

The principal significance of this plant is its fruit, which is a prime morsel for many woodland inhabitants: bears, birds, chipmunks, and other small mammals. The berries are also enjoyed by man, and even today are considered excellent when dried. Though the seeds impart a somewhat nutty taste, the berries themselves are quite bland and tasteless when eaten raw. Early frontiersmen and native Americans made a staple called pemmican from the berries and dried buffalo meat.

This plant is a vigorous invader of grassland areas commonly found near oaks, and is one of the first shrubby species to spring up in burned-over areas; a result of its ability to withstand drier areas.

Members of the serviceberry group are found throughout the continental United States—one measure of the favor in which the berries are held by the birds of our land, who have scattered the seeds all across the country.

PACIFIC MADRONE
Arbutus menziesii
Are-*beaut*-us men-*zee*-zee-eye

Key Identifier. Peeling bark. Large evergreen leaves.

General Shape. The madrone does not conform to one general outline, but varies quite widely in shape, from tall to short and from wide to narrow. Trunks can be either straight or crooked. It is generally a medium-sized tree, 40 to 60 feet high, with an open, rather sparse look.

Leaves. Alternate, simple leaves are thick and leathery; shiny dark green on top, silvery white below. They are oval-shaped with a blunt tip; 2½ to 5 inches long and 2 to 3 inches wide. The madrone is in the same family as the rhododendron, and there is a great "family likeness" in the appearance of the leaves.

Flowers. Small, drooping, white, urn-shaped flowers, about ¼ inch, are grouped in long clusters, 5 to 6 inches long. Home gardeners will find the flowers like those of the heathers, which also belong to the same family.

Fruit. Red or orange fruits are round, berrylike, and about ½ inch in diameter. They resemble a miniature orange. Borne in clusters, each fruit sticking out on a stiff little stem.

Bark, Twigs. The brilliant color of the bark is the most memorable feature of this tree. New twigs are multi-colored, a mixture of red, green and orange. During the first winter they take on the characteristic shiny red-brown color that is almost metallic looking. The bark is very thin, and peels away in large flakes, revealing an underbark with greenish tones. The trunk is almost never completely round, but flattened and twisted.

The madrone is found in dry sites from sea level to 6000 feet elevation, and from the Cascade or Sierra foothills to the Pacific. It never seems to grow in dense stands; we are more likely to see a single tree or at most a small grove. It is often considered an understory tree, growing in competition with other species. It will tolerate drought but not deep shade. Depending on its location, and the available room to grow, it can be 20 to 80 feet high. One giant in Humboldt County, California, is 80 feet high and 126 feet wide.

The thin bark makes the tree especially vulnerable to fire damage. But even if burned, or cut down, the stumps sprout easily; the young saplings sprout from around the sides of the stump, forming a ring (called a crown) around the former tree. The wood of the tree is very brittle, and easily damaged by heavy snows. The brightly colored berries are popular with birds, particularly the band-tailed pigeon, which is thought to be the principal disseminator of its seeds. Berries are edible (though bland), but be cautious: the sharp seeds have been known to cause stomach cramps.

West Coast Indians brewed a tea from the bark or leaves to treat colds, to cure stomachache, even to treat stomach ulcers. Leaves were made into a lotion to treat sores and cuts, on horses as well as people. The wood of madrone is a beautiful red color that turns well and would make beautiful veneer and other woodworking materials. Up to now, though, it has not been commercially developed.

THE WILLOW FAMILY
Salix
Say-licks

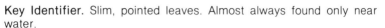

Key Identifier. Slim, pointed leaves. Almost always found only near water.

General Shape. Among the members of this large family, form varies from a tall tree to a tiny shrublet 6 inches high.

Leaves. Simple, alternate leaves are usually much longer than they are wide, with a long, tapering point. Most willows have a distinguishing pair of small "leaves," shaped like ears, at the base of the leaf stems.

Flowers. Flowers in elongated catkins, with tiny nectar glands. Flowers of each sex on a different tree. Insects seeking the nectar and, more importantly, wind pollinate the trees.

Fruit. Small green pear-shaped capsules, about ¼ inch long, are attached to a long stem. Each capsule contains a large number of tiny lightweight seeds that are easily and widely scattered by wind.

Bark, Twigs. Young twigs are extraordinarily tough, but often have a joint near their base so that they snap off easily. Larger stems are brittle and break easily but will withstand great compression.

More than 200 species of willow have been identified; they are widely scattered throughout the world and more than 100 species are native to North America, over ⅓ of them in the West. About 40 species reach a size that qualifies them as a tree; many are multi-stemmed shrubs of various heights; some are small plants only a few inches high. Except for a few of the very well-known trees, the willows are so similar in appearance that only a well-trained and well-equipped botanist can distinguish between the species. . .and even they have a difficult time of it. This is because different willow species can interbreed, producing an unbelievable number of combinations of characteristics.

Be content know you have a willow at hand.

Willows are most common along stream banks; here willow thickets may form an impenetrable barrier. There are a small number of sub-alpine species, which can subsist with little water; they seldom reach large size.

All willows grow quickly and have a short life span. They propagate readily by sprouting stems or roots from stumps. Their thickly matted root system performs a valuable function in preventing soil erosion along stream banks.

Native American tribes wove strips of the bark together into a twine. Because the willows are so prolific, and short-lived, using them for firewood is relatively nondestructive. Modern outdoorsmen are advised to watch for willow logs for camp use.

CALIFORNIA MYRTLE
Myrica californica
Mih-*rye*-ka *cal*-if-*or*-ni-ca

Key Identifier. Waxy fruit, resinous dotted leaves.

General Shape. A shrubby or low bushy tree. Trunk is short and branches are slender and upright, and create a narrow crown with a rounded top.

Leaves. Oblong shape, 2 to 4 inches long and about ½ inch wide. Margin, which may be toothed or smooth, curls under. A very dark glossy green on top, with a light yellow-green below; underside also covered with small black resin dots. There is a light resinous odor, very aromatic, released when leaves are crushed; it's mildly perceptible even without bruising. The evergreen leaves remain on the tree about one year, then fall individually.

Flowers. Male and female flowers occur in long catkins on same tree; they grow from the base where last year's leaves were found.

Fruit. A small (¼ inch) purple berry, thinly coated with a gray granular wax. Fruits mature in September and most fall in the winter, with some hanging on the tree till spring. Inside the flesh of the fruit is a single nut, with a very hard and thick shell.

Bark. Smooth gray-brown bark is a deep reddish-brown on the inside.

Another instance of conflicting common names: this tree is known as bayberry, wax myrtle, sweet gale, and California myrtle. . .and it isn't a myrtle at all!

This is a small tree, usually 8 to 20 feet; it also occurs as a shrub less than 5 feet high. In 25 years, it will develop a diameter of 6 inches.

This wax myrtle grows along the coastline from Washington to southern California. It plays an important role in the succession sequence in which coastal sand dunes are changed to stable forest.

The berries of this tree are food for the chestnut-backed chickadee, the Audubon and myrtle warbler, and the wren tit.

The wax from the berries of a similar species on the East Coast was once used for making bayberry-scented candles and soap.

62

CALIFORNIA LAUREL
Umbellularia californica
Oom-*bell*-you-*lair*-ee-ah *cal*-if-*or*-ni-ca

Key Identifier. Crush a few leaves in your hand; the odor of camphor tells you it's California laurel. The fruit resembles a yellow-green olive. This is an evergreen.

General Shape. When growing in the open, the tree has an extremely dense, round or elliptical crown; it looks a lot like a lollipop. Sometimes, they are found in thickets of dense, low trees, 10 to 15 feet high. In a dense forest, the trunk may be tall, clean and straight with a narrow crown of closely packed, small, upright branches.

Leaves. Glossy evergreen leaves are dark green on top, light green below. They are simple, alternate, and 3 to 5 inches long by ¾ to 1½ inches wide, with a thick, leathery texture. Leaves contain an oil which gives off a pungent odor like camphor when they are crushed; inhaled deeply, it can cause slight pain (though temporary) in the sinuses.

Fruit. Quite fleshy, shaped like an olive, 1 inch long. It's yellow-green when young, with purple splotches, purplish-brown when mature. Fruits produce one large seed.

Bark. Gray-brown and smooth when young, becoming dark reddish-brown and scaly with age.

The battle of the names: the recognized common name is California laurel; in southern Oregon it's known as Oregon myrtle; speaking botanically, it's neither a laurel nor a myrtle, but an entirely separate species.

It's normally a rather small tree, 30 to 40 feet high, although heights of 80 feet are not uncommon in heavy forests. A diameter of 25 inches may indicate an age of 200 years.

The myrtle/laurel requires a damp soil, and so is often found growing along streams, where the seeds may drop and float down large distances. It grows in dense clumps and patches, or can be scattered singly. A shade-tolerant tree, it's often found growing in small groups with bigleaf maple.

The leaves of this tree were brewed into a tea by trappers of the Hudson's Bay Company, to cure a chill.

Generations of Western woodworkers have prized this wood for its excellent properties; it's hard, firm, fine-grained, a rich color, and takes working exceedingly well. Note, for instance, that the golden spike which linked the transcontinental railroad was driven into a tie made from this wood. This is the tree that produces the famous "Oregon myrtlewood" boxes, tableware, and planters so prevalent at Western tourist shops.

64

OREGON ASH
Fraxinus latifolia
Frax-in-us lat-i-*foal*-ee-ah

Key Identifier. Leaf form: one of the few native Western trees with compound leaves. Single winged seed is shaped like the blade of a canoe paddle.

General Shape. When grown in the forest, this medium-sized tree has a long, clean trunk and a narrow, short crown of small branches. When it grows in the open, it has a short, thick trunk and wide, rounded crown with low-spreading branches. The branching pattern is opposite, an unusual feature of broadleaf trees. This can be a surefire way to identify the ash even in winter: the bare branches particularly show the opposite branching pattern. Old branches break with a hollow snap.

Leaves. Compound leaves are 5 to 14 inches long overall, and have 5 or 7 (occasionally 9) leaflets—always an odd number. The leaf stalk is thick and has a groove along the top. The leaflets are 3 to 7 inches long and 1½ inches wide, basically oval in shape with a sharp point at the end. They are pale green on top, even paler underneath, with a prominent midrib vein. Autumn color is yellow.

Flower. Male and female flowers on separate trees. Flowers are small and not important to identification.

Fruit. Single seeds are carried in dense clusters. Each has a wing 1½ inches long, shaped like the paddle of a canoe.

Bark. Bark is criss-crossed with deep seams, like a closely woven net.

The Oregon ash is usually found in wet or moist sites with rich soil, along stream banks or river benches and terraces. It is abundantly spread through the Pacific states, but does not grow very densely in any one place. The largest known tree is 79 feet high and 66 feet wide.

The wood of this tree was used by Western Indians for canoe paddles and for digging sticks. They brewed a tea from its bark that was thought to cure worms. Indians and early white hunters alike believed that no poisonous snakes would live where the ash tree grew, and that a stick made from the tree would make any rattlesnake retreat in fear.

Because the trees are so scattered, their commercial value is limited. The wood of ash trees is well-suited for furniture, flooring, skis, oars, paneling, and tool handles, but these items are commonly manufactured from Eastern varieties of ash, more abundant than our species. Ash wood makes an excellent fuel.

WESTERN CHINKAPIN
Castanopsis chrysophylla
Cass-tah-*nop*-sis *cry*-so-*fill*-ah

Key Identifier. Its unforgettable fruit, an incredibly spiny burr. Bottom and top of leaf two different colors: top is bright green, bottom is golden yellow.

General Shape. A small to medium-sized tree which if in the open grows straight, with a bushy crown that reaches almost to ground. If forest grown, the trunk leans toward sunlight and crown foliage is high in tree and lumped toward light.

Leaves. Spearpoint-shaped, 2 to 4 inches long and 1 to 1½ inches wide; leathery texture; deep mossy green color above. Leaf stem and bottom of leaf are covered with tiny golden-yellow scales, giving the tree its other common name, "golden chinkapin." Margins are smooth and curl under.

Flower. Small creamy white flowers, in 2-inch-long catkins, appear in early summer, and sometimes continue through midwinter. They are wind-pollinated.

Fruit. A very spiny burr, 1 to 1¾ inches in diameter, matures in autumn of the second year after pollination. It splits open, releasing a shiny, yellow-brown, sweet-tasting nut. Because of the sharp spines, few humans have tasted the nut, but squirrels and chipmunks have. . . often.

Bark. On young trees, bark is thin, smooth and dark gray. On mature trees, it is about 1 inch thick, deeply grooved into large plates which are reddish brown outside and brilliant red on the inside surface.

The chinkapin is a broad-leafed evergreen that is adapted to dry climates and grows well in rocky, gravelly soils. It is commonly found in mixed stands of Douglas fir, white fir and ponderosa pine on mountain slopes or sheltered ravines and gulleys. Pure, dense stands are not uncommon. In such areas it normally has a mature height of 30 to 50 feet with an 8 to 35-inch diameter. It also grows at higher elevations, as much as 8000 to 10,000 feet, where it takes the form of a low shrub.

It tolerates shade, but needs direct overhead sun to develop a long, straight trunk. In shaded circumstances it becomes subordinate to the taller associates and forms a distinct subcanopy. Largest living is 127 feet high, 5 feet 10 inches thick.

Because of its fairly small size, the chinkapin is a popular tree for home landscaping. As a commercial wood, it provides an excellent, although limited, source of good saw timber, used mainly for plywood or furniture manufacturing. The wood is fine-grained, fairly soft, and is considered brittle.

WESTERN DOGWOOD
Cornus nutallii
Corn-us *nut*-ah-lie

Key Identifier. Its familiar flower and distinctive leaf.

General Shape. Dogwood's form is governed by its location and habitat. In the forest, it is an understory tree or shrub, usually 20 to 30 feet high, with slender trunk and branches. The leaves cluster at the ends of the branches, giving the forest dogwood an open, almost bare appearance. In the open, it can assume large tree proportions, with a thick trunk, massive branches, and dense foliage.

Leaves. Simple, opposite leaves are oval-shaped with a pointed tip. The veins, which are deeply depressed into the leaf, curve outward to follow the shape of the leaf. Margins are somewhat wavy. Leaves are 4 to 6 inches long and 2 to 3 inches wide. In fall they turn orange to deep purplish-red, commonly bright red.

Flowers. What we think of as the dogwood flower—the brilliant white petals—is in reality a cluster of bracts (modified leaves); the true flowers are tiny green-white blossoms tucked inside the bracts. Each "flower" has 4 to 6 bracts. The Western dogwoods frequently bloom in both spring and fall, particularly if the fall weather is mild.

Fruit. Small red fruits are grouped in tight, dense clusters. They are about ½ inch long, oval-shaped, with a flattened end.

Bark. Bark is thin, brown, and smooth; very old trees develop tight scales in the bark.

The beautiful dogwood grows almost everywhere there is Douglas fir. With its striking flowers in the spring and bright fall color, it provides a brilliant accent in the deep green forests of the West.

Because dogwoods are not inhibited by shade, they grow quite well as an understory tree in dense forests. We normally see them as individual trees, or in small groups. The largest known living tree (in Clatskanie, Oregon) is 50 feet high, 50 feet wide, and has a trunk that is 3 feet 5 inches thick.

The fruit of the Western dogwood is favored by many songbirds, in particular the band-tailed pigeon. It is this attraction that led to the naming of the tree by the famed naturalist, Audubon. When a specimen of this pigeon was sent to him by a colleague of the botanist Thomas Nuttall, who was Audubon's friend, Audubon decided to include a depiction of the tree in his painting of the band-tailed pigeon for the famous *Birds of America*. As it was Nuttall who had discovered the tree in an 1834 expedition to the Northwest, Audubon felt it appropriate to name the tree in honor of his friend.

Indians of the Northwest used the wood (hardened by drying) to make harpoons for salmon fishing. Bark, scraped off and boiled into a tea, was used as a general tonic by several tribes; physicians of some of the early explorations used this bark tea in place of quinine to cure Indian children of malaria. Aside from its occasional use as an ornamental tree, the Western dogwood has no significant commercial use today. Its value is perhaps the joy it brings to all who see it.

QUAKING ASPEN
Populus tremuloides
Pop-you-*lus trim*-you-*loy*-deez

Key Identifier. White bark. Thin, flat petioles set perpendicular to the leaf.

General Shape. Usually, tree has a tall, straight trunk with horizontal branches forming a narrow, round crown. Trunk is almost same diameter for at least half its length; branches are irregularly bent. On dry, exposed locations, trunk may be short and twisted.

Leaf. Simple, alternate leaves are almost circular, with a slight point; 1 to 3 inches in diameter, with small, rounded teeth on the margins. Lustrous green on top and silvery below; autumn color is a brilliant yellow. The petiole is flat, as if it had been pinched in along its entire length; it is attached at right angles to the plane of the leaf. This unique feature causes the leaf to flutter in the slightest breeze.

Flower. Male and female flowers are on separate trees, in the form of droopy, hairy catkins; they are pollinated by wind.

Fruit. Small green capsules, 1/4 inch long, in long clusters. Each capsule contains many small brown seeds, so tiny that it takes 3 million of them to make a pound. Each seeds has tufts of silky hair. Seeds are often sterile.

Bark. Thin, smooth and white or cream-colored; it often appears broken and marked with black patches and scars.

This beautiful tree, which needs only 7 inches of water per year, is the most widely spread tree species on the North American continent. It tolerates an incredibly wide range of temperatures, from $-78°$ in Alaska to $+110°$ in Arizona. It grows from sea level to 6000 feet in the far North and to 10,000 feet in the southern part of its range. It's a relatively small tree, with a common mature height of 30 to 40 feet with a trunk diameter of 8 to 12 inches. The largest living tree is 109 feet high and 2 feet 10 inches thick.

Aspens are members of the poplar family, which are ancient trees known to have existed 75 million years ago. Today they play a particularly important role in forest ecology. Though many aspen seeds are sterile or weak, the enormous numbers blown from distant aspen stands provide the first trees to appear in burned-out or cleared land. If aspen had been there previously, root suckers may produce even more trees than seeds. The new trees grow quickly and produce a large number of leaves, which improve the soil as they fall and decay. Also, because the seeds germinate well on wet soil, the trees grow easily along stream banks, where they act as soil stablizers.

The aspen is a food source for a host of friendly insects, and its inner bark, though bitter to our taste, is the very favorite food of beavers. Bark, buds, twigs and leaves are eaten by rabbits and deer.

The wood of the aspen is soft, lightweight, brittle and decays quickly. It is used for paper, pulpwood, and wooden matches; because the wood itself has no odor, it is an important source of material for vegetable crates.

BLACK COTTONWOOD
Populus trichocarpa
Pop-you-lus *try*-ko-*carp*ah

Key Identifier. Leaf shape (like an egg with a sharp point) and the characteristic terminal bud: long, curving, covered with a sweet-smelling yellow-brown gum.

General Shape. In a dense stand, the trunk is long and clear of branches for much of its height, with a narrow, open crown of short branches. When grown in the open, the tree has the same long clean trunk, which is clear of limbs for half its height.

Leaves. Simple, alternate leaves are oval or egg-shaped, tapering to a sharp point; 3 to 5 inches long. Thick and leathery, with fine teeth on the margins, with conspicuous veins. Dark shiny green above, silvery white below, with some rust-colored areas underneath.

Flowers. Male and female flowers on separate trees; both in the form of a drooping, rather hairy catkin. Appear in early spring before leaves.

Fruit. Small, almost round, somewhat hairy green capsules develop on catkins where flowers were. Each capsule contains tiny, woolly, tufted seeds, and there are *zillions* of them on each tree. The tiny seeds are carried long distances by wind or water, and at their season cover the ground like cotton. They germinate best in wet river bottoms.

Bark, Twigs. Young bark is smooth and gray or greenish-yellow; on mature trees, becomes 2 inches thick, dark gray and deeply grooved. New twigs have rather angular sides, but become round as they grow older. The terminal bud (at the very end of the twig) is about ¾ inch long and tapers to a long, gently curving point. It is yellowish and thicker than its twig. The bud is coated with a fragrant gum, which gives the tree the common name of "balsam poplar" or "balsam cottonwood."

This tree is always found growing near water—either surface water, like streams, or underground water. It prefers a humid climate, as in the Northwest, and tolerates very cold winters. It requires sunlight, does not tolerate shade.

It's a particularly fast-growing tree, which means that it always stands taller than associates and is the first to suffer wind damage. In the spring, heavy frosts will crack the bark and limbs, allowing diseases to enter. Also susceptible to fire damage.

The cottonwood will reach its mature height, 50 feet, in 60 years, with a diameter of 24 to 30 inches. A tree 100 years old will have a diameter of about 3 feet. The largest living is 147 feet high, 9.61 feet thick, in Yamhill County, Oregon.

Black cottonwood was especially significant to pioneers traveling westward, for two reasons: it was often the only shade for miles around, and, catching sight of a cottonwood from a distance, they would know a water source was likely.

Today, the wood is used as lumber, as plywood, as veneer, and to manufacture boxes and barrels. When used in home landscaping, only the male trees are planted, to avoid the troublesome cottony seeds loosed by the female.

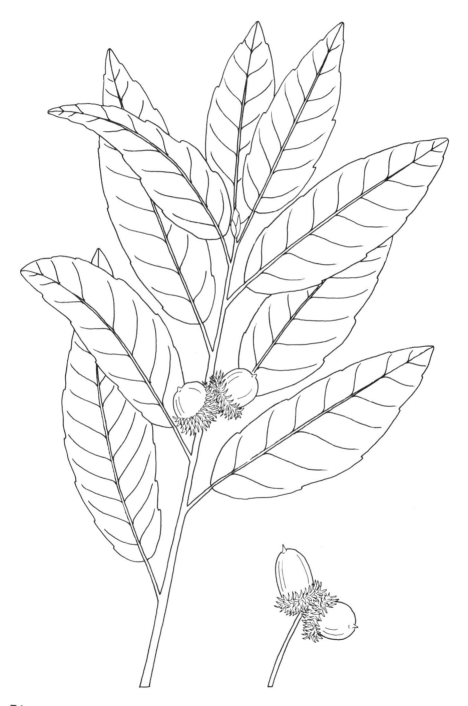

74

TANOAK
Lithocarpus densiflorus
Lith-oh-*carp*-us den-si-*floor*-us

Key Identifier. Acorn cup has spiny bristles. Leaves are thick, fuzzy, and evergreen—unlike true oaks.

General Shape. Form of the tanoak is widely variable, depending on the environment in which it grows. In ideal conditions, it can be 60 to 100 feet high and 1 to 3 feet in diameter, with a crown shaped into a narrow pyradmid by ascending branches.

Leaves. Simple, alternate leaves are thick and leathery. Leaves stay on the tree 3 to 4 years. This is an evergreen. Leaves are 3 to 5 inches long and 1 to 2½ inches wide, roughly oval in shape, with blunt teeth on the margins and a blunt tip. They are light green, smooth and shiny on top; underside is covered with very dense, rust-colored hairs, giving the leaf a fuzzy texture.

Flowers. Flowers resemble those of chestnuts and chinkapins (see page 67. Tiny white, ill-smelling blossoms on a narrow catkin, 3 to 4 inches long. They appear in spring, may persist as long as August. There are many flowers (*densiflorus* means "densely flowered").

Fruit. The fruit of the tanoak is a long, hard acorn (*Lithocarpus* means "stone fruit"). They are carried on a long, hairy stalk, either singly or in sets of 2 or 3; the cups are shallow and covered with tough, pointed bristles. Each tree produces an enormous number of fruits.

Bark, Twigs. Young twigs have a coating of woolly hairs, but these are lost in the first year and stems become smooth and dark reddish-brown. Bark of young trees is mottled, smooth and gray. As the trees mature, the bark becomes broken by narrow seams into squarish plates. The bark is up to 5 inches thick.

There are some 100 species of *Lithocarpus* recorded, but most of them are in southeastern Asia. Only one species is native to America, and it is found only in California and southern Oregon. The tanoak requires ocean fogs to survive. It is most often found in association with redwoods, but also will grow on poor, stony soil if moisture is abundant. Here the tree will have a twisted, stunted shape. At Knee-land, California, the largest tanoak rises to a height of 100 feet. Normally, trees are 50 to 90 feet high with a 9 to 24-inch diameter. Tanoaks are relatively long-lived: a tree with a 12-inch diameter may be 100 years old.

Acorns are popular food for rodents and small mammals, and also for insects, who infect half of the acorns produced. Woodpeckers, jays, and many other birds also enjoy the acorns.

The bark of tanoak is rich in tannin, an acid. Rain leaches the acid from dead leaves and bark, creating a special soil condition which is thought by some scientists to be a stimulant to the growth of red-woods.

The tannin, which is used in tanning hides, at one time gave the tanoak a commercial prominence. In recent years, sources of low-cost tannin from abroad have reduced the demand for tanoak bark.

CALIFORNIA BLACK OAK
Quercus kelloggii
Quirk-us *kell*-og-eye

Key Identifier. Tips of leaves are sharply pointed and stiff. Leaning trunks are common.

General Shape. From a short distance, the high, rounded crown and dark green pointed leaves give this tree a certain resemblance to the maples. Often the trunk is bent, or the entire tree leans slightly. Branches are large and point stiffly upward.

Leaves. This can be a frustrating tree to identify, for leaves of different shapes are often found on the same tree. In general terms, however, leaves are 3 to 6 inches long and 2 to 3 inches wide with 5 to 7 lobes. The tips of the lobes are very sharp spines. When leaves first appear in spring, they are tinged with red. In autumn, they turn yellow.

Fruit. Produces large numbers of acorns, which mature at the end of the second season. They are a pale chestnut color, with a deep cup. The cup has thin, shiny, rough scales outside and a mat of tangly woolly hairs inside. Normally acorns are about 1½ inches long, but size can vary widely on the same tree.

Bark, Twigs. The name "black oak" comes from the bark color: a deep brownish black on mature trees. Bark is very hard and deeply seamed near the bottom of the trunk. Bark of young trees is smooth and dull gray-brown. New-growth twigs are clear red or red-brown, smooth, with a whitish tint.

This rugged tree likes a warm, dry climate, and grows most often on mountain slopes and elevated canyons up to 5000 feet. It forms wide, open stands, either pure or mixed with other species; a grove of black oak creates a serene, parklike atmosphere.

California black oak is a medium-sized tree; generally 50 to 70 feet high with 15 to 30 inches diameter. A 20-inch tree may be 200 years old. Mature trees are quite vulnerable to decay; a deeply hollowed trunk usually indicates a very old tree. Largest living is 124 feet high, 115 feet across and almost 9 feet thick.

Though California black oak acorns are bitter to taste, they are the favorite food of the acorn woodpecker of California and southern Oregon. During seasons of low acorn yield, this bird drills holes into the sides of trees, telephone poles, fence posts and almost anything else that resembles a tree, and then hammers a California black oak acorn into the hole—pointed end first—till the bottom is flush. No animal, including squirrels and chipmunks, can rob this cache, assuring a sufficient supply for the winter.

Northern California Indians prized the wood of this tree as a fuel for drying seeds, as it burns slowly, without much flame. Today, its primary commercial value is as a fuel, although the wood has much potential for furniture and flooring.

77

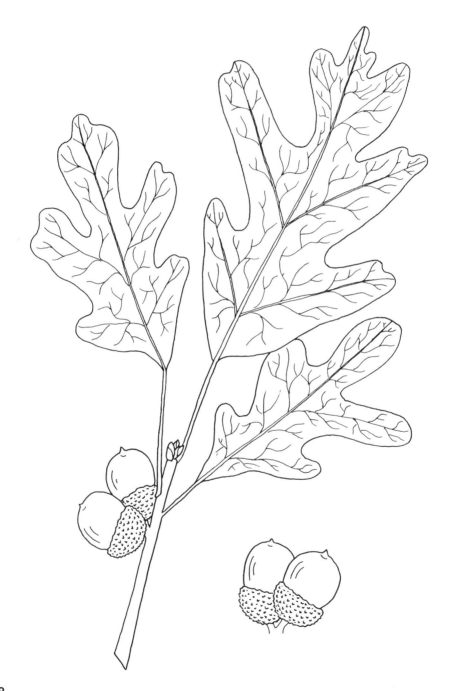

OREGON WHITE OAK
Quercus garryana
Quirk-us gary-*aye*-na

Key Identifier. Leaf shape: tips of the lobes are rounded, not pointed.

General Shape. A medium-sized tree with a short, thick trunk and a broad, round-topped crown of heavy, gnarled limbs. In the open, trees have a very regular, spherical shape that looks trimmed.

Leaves. Alternate, simple, 3 to 6 inches long and 3 to 4 inches wide. With 5 to 7 rounded lobes, deeply curved in; the center lobe has a rather squarish end. Margins curl under slightly. Deep green, shiny and smooth on top, pale green or orange-brown and hairy underneath. Very undistinguished fall color. Dead brown leaves persist on tree well into winter.

Flowers. Insignificant flowers in early summer. Both sexes occur on the same tree: the male is a hairy catkin, female is single or double blossom. The flower is not an important factor in identification.

Fruit. Acorn is 1 to 1 ¼ inches long, oblong, with a bowllike scaly cup embracing one-third of its length. Cup scales are hairy and have a free, pointed tip. This species often has acorns of different sizes occurring on the same tree.

Bark, Twigs. Young twigs and limbs have smooth gray bark. Bark on mature trees has wide, vertical ridges and narrow horizontal furrows, which gives a mosaic pattern. Twigs are thick, orange-red, and hairy in their first season.

Oregon white oak is a slow-growing tree; its best climate is humid, with soil which is more often dry than wet. It is common on grassy, well-drained slopes, in southern or southwestern exposures, at elevations of up to 4000 feet.

This tree is often found as individuals, or in small groups surrounded by grass. Dispersion is thought to be the result of the small animals' storing acorns in scattered caches. Pure stands do occur and are notable because they are thought to be inadvertently caused by white man. Prior to settlement, wide-ranging ground fires were common. These kept the shrub cover down and killed off much of the oak seedling crop. With fires controlled, oak forests are developing.

White oak usually reaches a height of about 50 feet with a diameter of 12 to 30 inches. It may take 180 years to reach a diameter of 18 inches. Largest living is 98 feet high, 72 feet across, and 7 feet thick.

Young seedlings are vulnerable to damage of summer drought, and to grass fires. Physical damage from grazing and trampling also takes its toll, but few serious diseases trouble the white oak.

The acorn, as we all know, is meat and potatoes to pocket gophers, deer, mice, chipmunks, and squirrels, who often consume an entire year's crop. Grazing cattle nibble at the leaves, which have a very high protein content. In a pinch for feed, farmer have fed white oak branches to their stock.

The wood of white oak, although very strong and durable, is not commercially important. It's a popular tree for home landscaping.

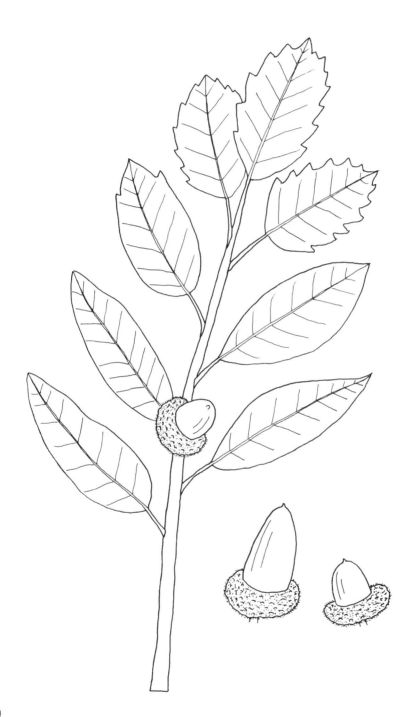

CANYON LIVE OAK
Quercus chrysolepis
Quirk-us *chris*-oh-*lep*-is

Key Identifier. Two kinds of leaves on same branch; golden hair on outside of acorn cup. This is an evergreen.

General Shape. Form of tree varies greatly, from a low, dense chapparal shrub to a large, high tree with a short, crooked trunk and a wide crown of massive limbs.

Leaves. New leaves, whether those on young trees or the new season's growth on an older tree, are distinctly different from mature leaves. Juvenile leaves have very sharp teeth on the margin, giving them a look almost like holly. They also have a yellowish fuzz on the underside, which is lost in time. These new leaves slowly change, filling in between the teeth, so that mature leaves have smooth margins, with no teeth; and the leaf is a pale blue-green underneath. They are oblong ovals, thick, shiny, leathery in texture, yellow-green, and 1 to 4 inches long and ½ to 1 inch wide. Leaves stay on the tree 3 to 4 years, do not shed in autumn.

Fruit. This tree produces a large crop of acorns. Most are about 1½ inches long and roughly oval in shape, but size and shape varies. Pale chestnut color, often with downy hair on the point of the acorn. The cups may be either thin or very thick, but all are densely covered with a yellow or yellow-white wool, so thick that it hides the cup scales.

Bark, Twigs. Mature bark is black, ridged, and scaly-looking. Year-old twigs are red-brown and covered with dense woolly hair.

Canyon live oaks prefer dry areas, and thrive on steep, rocky slopes, canyon bottoms or rolling foothills. The form of the tree is very much determined by amount of water available during its growing years, the soil condition, and the space available. Mature oaks may vary from a low shrub to a tall tree. Generally, a mature tree will be 30 to 40 feet high and 30 to 60 inches in diameter. It's a very long-lived tree: a 10-inch diameter may indicate a 100-year-old tree. Largest living is 72 feet tall, more than 11 feet thick, and 80 feet across, in the Cleveland National Forest, California. Live oaks are sometimes found in pure stands, but more often intermixed with other oaks or with dry-area pines.

The acorn of this, as of other oaks, is an enormously popular food for almost all small forest animals. In the same way, it was an important food source for most Indian tribes, who ground it into flour.

The wood of the live oak is very heavy, strong, and durable; it was much sought after for wagon tongues and cross bars, wheel stock and axles, and was favored by pioneers for the head of mauls. Today it is a popular ornamental.

81

REDWOOD
Sequoia sempervirens
See-*quoy*-ah sem-pur-*vie*-rens

Key Identifier. Two kinds of leaves on the same branch: needles in two flat rows, and very short needles all around the stem.

General Shape. Young trees have a sharply pointed crown with branches that droop to the ground; overall, a thick and bushy plant. Mature trees have a tall, narrow, cone-shaped crown and branches that hang downward; this gives the crown the shape of a spear tip. The oldest branches stand out rigidly.

Leaves. Needles are a very shiny and dark yellow-green, ½ to 1 inch long, flat, and with a pointed tip. They are attached singly to the branches on a base that lies flat against the stem and pulls off with a tear rather than a clean break. Needles grow in two ways, on the same branch. Those on the side twigs are clearly two-ranked and extend straight out from the stem, while those on the primary branch lie quite close to the stem, some quite short and overlapped like scales.

Flowers. This tree flowers in the winter (blossoms are insignificant), and is pollinated by wind.

Fruit. Cones are small (¾ to 1 inch long), reddish brown, and grow from the ends of the branchlets. They mature in the autumn after winter flowering, open and loose seeds during the winter; cones may stay on the tree several months after opening. Seeds are very small, and have such small wings that they are barely moved by the wind, but tend to plummet straight to the ground.

Bark, Roots. Bark is reddish brown, fibrous, and deeply grooved; on old trees, it may be 12 inches thick. The tree has no taproot, but a wide network of side roots.

The California redwood requires a very specific set of environmental conditions: it grows exclusively along the Pacific Coast where coastal fogs provide a humid atmosphere during the summer. It is rarely found above 3000 feet and never on ocean-facing slopes, for salt blown in by the wind causes fatal damage.

The thick bark's protection against fire contributes to its huge size and is a cause in the growth of nearly pure stands of mature trees. When mature, redwoods are usually 200 to 250 feet high with a diameter of 8 to 10 feet. The largest living tree, in Humboldt State Park in California, is 362 feet high and 16 feet 8 inches thick. It is recorded that a tree 21 feet thick was nearly 1400 years old.

Redwood stumps have the unusual ability to sprout new trees. Trees badly damaged or killed by fire or disease will put forth sprouts in a ring all around and next to the stump. This ring looks like and is often called a "crown of sprouts." Redwood is generally free of serious diseases, except for a root rot which enters through burn scars.

Redwood is a very significant commercial wood, important for both interior and exterior construction. It is especially useful where wood must be used in direct contact with the ground, as in foundations, beams, and posts.

83

PACIFIC YEW
Taxus brevifolia
Tax-us brev-ah-*foal*-ee-ah

Key Identifier. Dark, dark green needles and bright red berrylike fruit.

General Shape. A small tree (20 to 30 feet) with dense foliage. The crown is conical and composed of slender, horizontally spreading branches which bear many flat, often drooping branchlets. In the open, branches may extend down trunk nearly to ground. In heavy forests, yew is often a squat, shrubby tree sprawling under the larger trees with a twisted trunk and no particular shape to the branches.

Leaves. Needles are short, ½ to 1 inch long, slender, sharply pointed, very dark green above and somewhat lighter below. They are attached to the branch on a thin threadlike stem that tears cleanly away from the twig. They are arranged in two ranks, somewhat like grand fir (except grand fir needles are not sharp) and similar to redwood (except that redwood needles do not have the thin stem).

Fruit. The unique fruit is a bright red cup-shaped "berry," encircling a single, bone-hard greenish seed. Fruit is produced only on female trees, and a nearby male tree is a necessity.

Bark. Thin (¼ inch) and papery, reddish-purple bark easily flakes away, revealing a clear red inner bark.

The yew grows best in moist, dark forests at low to medium elevations. It can even be found in dry areas, clustered along the edges of streams. It is abundant throughout its range, but never occurs in dense patches. This small tree is remarkably tolerant of shade, and is part of the understory in all but the darkest of forests.

The largest known Pacific yew is only 60 feet high; for many of the other tree species of our Western forests, 60 feet is next to nothing. The yew is a slow grower as well; it may take 90 years to reach a trunk diameter of 6 inches.

The fruit is very popular with birds, who are unable to digest the hard seeds, which are therefore disseminated over a wide range. Humans should not experiment with the berries, however, as there is some evidence that they are poisonous.

Yew wood has long been used for bows, but it was also used by native Americans for many other things: paddles, harpoon and spear shafts, cooking utensils, spoons, etc. Because the wood is very tough, it was thought to possess special qualities; teas brewed from the needles were believed to give strength to young and old. Leaves mashed into a pulp were used as a poultice for wounds, and bark tea was considered a lung medicine.

In spite of its toughness, the scarcity of yew almost precludes commercial use today. A very durable material, it is often used locally for gate posts, fence posts, and other uses where decay-resistance is important.

WESTERN HEMLOCK
Tsuga heterophylla
soo-gah het-ur-oh-*fill*-ah

Key Identifier. Drooping leader, tiny cones, and small, light-green needles in double-file arrangement on the branches. See page 89 for hemlock comparisons.

General Shape. A narrow, tall, graceful pyramid atop a long, straight, smooth trunk. The tip of the tree droops over and all branch ends arch slightly upward, then curve down. Once you know the shape of this graceful tree, it is virtually impossible to mistake. Overall, a soft, feathery texture.

Leaves. Needles are small (¼ to ¾ inch), single, glossy, and yellow-green. They have a groove down the topside and a distinctly blunt tip; are flat in cross-section. Needles appear to be growing in two opposite rows on the upper side of the twigs. Because the needles are so small, the branches have a thin, airy look.

Fruit. Very small cones (¾ to 1¼ inches) are oval-shaped, light brown, and pendent. Cones often show on trees as young as 20 years, but they will have no seeds until the tree is 25 or 30. The seeds are small with large wings, and often dispersed a long way from the parent tree. Each cone has about 40 seeds, but relatively few of them are fertile.

Bark, Twigs. New-growth twigs are slightly hairy. Bark of young trees is russet brown; on older trees, a darker brown in flat, scaly ridges.

This stately tree grows best in cool, wet areas of low elevation. Mature trees reach a height of 175 to 225 feet; they are very long-lived and slow-growing: a tree 16 inches in diameter may be 200 years old. The largest now living is 163 feet high, 62 inches across, 8 feet 8 inches thick in the Olympic National Forest.

The Western hemlock survives quite nicely in the shade of larger neighbors. Because it does not have the genetic need to outrace other trees for sunlight, it is usually seen as an understory tree, especially in association with sitka spruce and Douglas fir, and it does not normally form pure stands unless the more dominant trees have been removed.

The dense, low foliage of young trees provides excellent winter cover for grouse, wild turkey and deer; its abundant seeds are a food source for many birds and squirrels.

This was a versatile tree for Indians, who made a dye from its bark, used its pitch to prevent sunburn and chapping, and boiled the bark into a healing tea for sore throats or as a laxative. It is the state tree of Washington.

Western hemlock makes the very finest paper fibers; it also produces a superior lumber used in flooring, siding, and interior paneling. Gym floors are often made of hemlock because of its high resistance to scratches.

MOUNTAIN HEMLOCK
Tsuga mertensiana
Soo-gah murr-*ten*-see-*ann*-ah

Key Identifier. Dark green needles arranged in spirals all around the stem, giving the appearance of starry clusters. See species comparisons below.

General Shape. In dense forests, the crown is a slender, narrow-bottomed pyramid, with branches starting from about halfway up the trunk and curving downward. Trees grown in the open have a somewhat broader crown and branches quite far down the trunk, to within a few feet of the ground. Has the drooping tip and arching branches characteristic of hemlocks.

Leaves. Bluish-green needles (darker than Western hemlock) are ½ to 1 inch long and round in cross-section. Single needles are attached in spirals all around the stems. When the tree is viewed from a slight distance, the needles seem to be set in starry clusters placed at random on the branches.

Fruit. Cones are small, ½ to 3 inches, cylindrical, and hang down from the branches. They vary in color from yellow-green to purplish; color is not a dependable key to identification. A new crop of cones is produced each year, and so many that the branches seem to bend under their weight.

Bark. Dark reddish-brown bark is rough and ridged, even on young trees.

The durable mountain hemlock should be considered a subalpine tree, typically found at higher elevations, associating with Pacific silver fir and subalpine fir. It thrives where the growing season is short and winters are long and cold with much snow. Generally found near timberline, it may grow in much lower elevations where the necessary harsh conditions exist. Particularly at higher elevations, seeds germinate on top of rotten logs, which then support young trees. Heavy snows bend young sapling trunks, but do not kill the tree; thereafter the trunk is permanently crooked.

This is a smaller tree than the Western hemlock, but retains the same gracefully curving branch patterns. Most mature trees are 50 to 100 feet high, with a 10 to 20 inch diameter. The largest living tree is 113 feet high and 7 feet thick.

Like other hemlocks, this tree tolerates deep shade very well; because of the heavy shade created by deep forests, it is often found as a low-growing plant in association with many of our native Western trees. Because its branches are low to the ground, the tree is highly vulnerable to fire.

TO DISTINGUISH BETWEEN HEMLOCKS	
Western	Found at low elevations. Taller tree. Very small cone. Needles are yellow-green, light-colored in comparison, and flat. They appear to grow in two even rows, on opposite sides of the stem.
Mountain	Found at high elevations or areas of severe winters. Shorter tree with thick trunk. Larger cone. Needles are bluish-green, comparatively darker, and rounded. Needles arranged in spirals all around the stem, giving the appearance of starry clusters set at random on the branch.

COLORADO BLUE SPRUCE
Picea pungens
Pie-*see*-ah *pun*-jenz

Key Identifier. Blue or blue-green color. See sitka spruce (page 95) for species comparisons.

General Shape. In the open, it is a fairly narrow pyramidal tree, with branches down the trunk almost to ground. Branches extend out in very regular tiers. In the forest, it is a medium-sized tree which loses lower branches; the trunk is tall and straight, and the crown has the same clean, pyramidal shape.

Leaves. Stiff, sharp needles are 1 to 1½ inches long and are attached all around the stem. They have a silvery blue cast, particularly new foliage, that is quite distinctive. Needles are diamond-shaped in cross-section.

Fruit. Cone is 2½ to 4½ inches long (larger than Englemann spruce and somewhat larger than sitka spruce), roughly cylindrical in shape, and hangs down from branches. Scales are stiff and spreading, with ragged margins. The seed is a dark chestnut brown, with a single wing.

Bark, Twig. Bark is ¾ to 1½ inches thick, deeply grooved. Twigs are stiff and thick, and vary from orange-brown to gray-brown.

Colorado blue spruce, best known for the silvery blue look of its young needles, grows abundantly on moist slopes and along streams of the Rocky Mountains. The stately spruce is so much a part of the visual character of Colorado, it is no surprise that it is designated the state tree.

This is a slow-growing tree, which usually reaches a mature height of 80 to 100 feet. The largest living tree of record is 126 feet high, has a spread of 36 feet and a trunk diameter of 4 feet 11 inches.

Blue spruce is used somewhat for poles, posts, and fuels, but its chief commercial significance is in the landscape industry. The lustrous blue foliage and the extremely regular, symmetrical shape have made this tree a favorite for home gardens, and several ornamental varieties have been developed especially for this purpose.

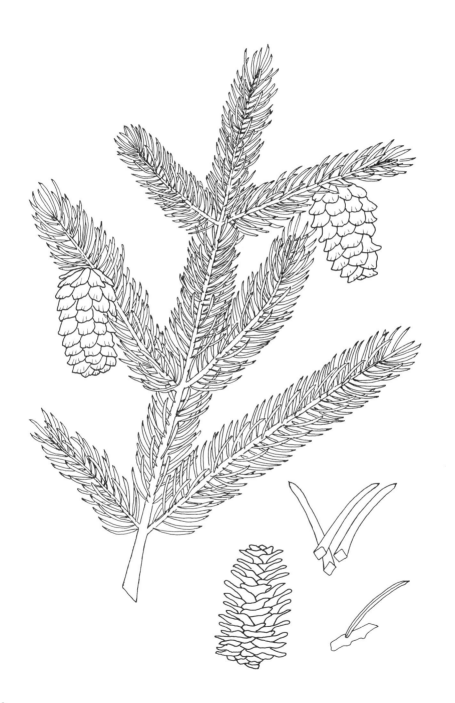

ENGELMANN SPRUCE
Picea engelmannii
Pie-*see*-ah *en*-gull-mun-eye

Key Identifier. Needles are stiff but blunt, and give off an unpleasant odor when crushed. See sitka spruce (page 95) for species comparisons.

General Shape. In thick stands, has a long, straight trunk with branches only at the top and a sharp, dense, pointed crown. On single trees, crowns are longer and wider; drooping branches often touch the ground. At very high altitudes, you might not even recognize the tree: it is about 3 feet high and spreads enormously long branches over the ground.

Leaves. All spruce needles are quite stiff, grow singly rather than in bundles, and are thickly attached all around the branch on a short woody base which stays on the stem when the needle is pulled off. Engelmann needles are a deep bluish-green, ½ to 1 inch long, blunt-tipped, square or rounded in cross-section; they often curve upward, so that when viewed from above, the needles *appear* to be growing from the top of the branch.

Fruit. Cones of all species hang downward from branches. Engelmann cones are small, about 1½ inches, slightly oval, cinnamon brown. Scales are very thin and flexible, and the dark brown seeds tucked deep between the scales are quite small, with a single wing.

Bark, Twigs. Reddish-brown, with small scales, like fish scales, which flake off easily. New twigs are slightly fuzzy.

The Engelmann spruce survives in the highest and coldest forest environment in the U.S. It can tolerate temperatures of -50°F, and is found (in the Rockies) as high as 11,000 feet. Along with subalpine fir and mountain hemlock, it is among the last trees before the timberline level. These trees frequently cluster in frost pockets; don't camp nearby unless you are prepared for cold.

At low elevations, mature trees are 100 to 150 feet high and 16 to 30 inches thick; trees 20 inches in diameter may be 400 years old. The largest living specimen is 179 feet high, 43 feet across, and 7 feet 8 inches thick.

The Engelmann is not deterred by shade, and often survives its taller and faster-growing companions. Dense, pure stands with no understory are common.

Because the tree has very thin bark, and because on younger trees, dead lower limbs hang on the tree for a long time, it is vulnerable to both fire and physical injury. In spite of a deep root system, it is susceptible to windthrow after a stand has been thinned.

The seeds of Engelmann spruce are a food source for many birds and small rodents, but because they are very tiny, most seeds are dispersed by the wind before anyone gets a chance at them.

Piano sounding boards are often made of Engelmann spruce. The wood is lightweight, fine-textured, and straight-grained, and makes a very fine construction lumber; trees are used for telephone poles.

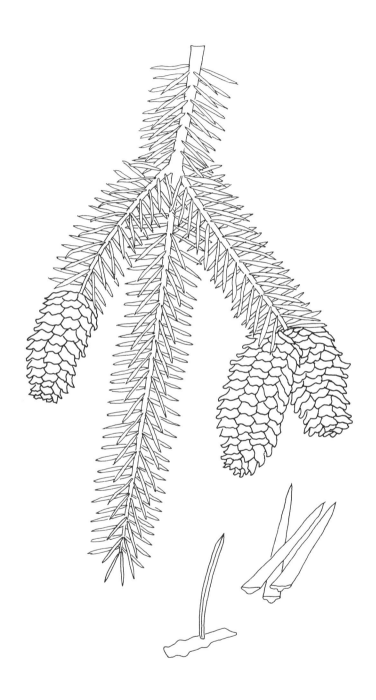

SITKA SPRUCE
Picea sitchensis
Pie-*see*-ah *sit*-ken-sis

Key Identifier. Very sharp, stiff needles, and its coastal location. See below for comparison of spruce species.

General Shape. Tall and conical, with a regular geometric shape. In open stands, the branches are long and grow from well down on the trunk, giving the pointed crown a broad base. The branches have an upward sweep at the ends, but the branches and twigs droop weepingly. In dense stands, branches are shorter and begin far up the trunk, creating a narrow, sharply pointed cone. Overall, a solid, rather heavy texture.

Leaves. Like all spruces, needles are stiff, attached singly all around the branch, like a bottle brush. Sitka needles are very sharp, light yellow-green, ½ to 1 ¼ inches long, and a very flat trapezoid in cross-section.

Fruit. Cone is 3 to 4 inches long (larger than Engelmann), varies in color from pale yellow to reddish brown, and, like all spruces, hangs downward from under the branch. Cone scales are thin and papery; the single-winged seeds are minute (210,000 to the pound) and easily dispersed by the wind.

Bark, Twigs. Mature bark is thin, reddish-brown, and breaks off in large scales. New twigs are smooth.

Sitka spruce is a coastal tree; except for the specialized climate zone of the Columbia River Gorge in Oregon and Washington, it rarely occurs more than 2 to 3 miles inland. It requires very high humidity, and will even grow in floodplains or tidelands where it is regularly inundated. If the soil is unstable, thick buttressed roots develop at the base of the trunk. It grows abundantly, and will crowd out the shore pine, which comes first in the vegetative succession, but which cannot tolerate shade. At maturity this tree is enormous: up to 180 feet high and 8 to 12 feet in diameter. The largest known living, near Seaside, Oregon, is 216 feet high and 16 feet 8 inches thick.

The sitka was much used by Northwest Indians. Woven roots were used in baskets, rainhats, and cord for tying; the inner bark was brewed for medicinal tea, good for sore throats; the new sprouts were eaten raw; and the pitch was used like chewing gum.

Sitka spruce has the highest strength-to-weight ratio of any timber. It is used for ladders, doors, oars, scaffolding, bleachers, and masts; also for vital parts of pianos, organs, and violins. When the skeletons of airplanes were made from wood, sitka spruce was the most sought-after material.

TO DISTINGUISH BETWEEN SPRUCES	
Colorado Blue	Largest cones. Blue-green needles. Found in Rockies.
Engelmann	Small, dark cones. Fuzzy twigs. Dark green needles, stiff but not sharp. Found in high mountain country. Unpleasant odor when crushed.
Sitka	Larger, lighter cones. Smooth twigs. Light green needles, sharp-pointed. Found only near seashore or Columbia Gorge. No unpleasant odor.

WESTERN LARCH
Laryx occidentalis
Lair-icks *oxy*-den-*tal*-iss

Key Identifier. Larches are the only needle-leaf trees in the West that change color with the seasons and lose their foliage in the winter. To compare larch species, see page 99.

General Shape. The trunk is very long and free of branches for much of its length; branches are short and almost exactly horizontal, with perhaps a slight droop. General texture is soft, almost lacy.

Leaves. Needles are 1 to 1¾ inches long, basically triangular in cross-section, and yellow-green. The new growth in spring is light apple green, becoming somewhat darker in summer. Needles occur on short spurs, in bunches of 12 to 40, although the new growth may appear singly. The woody spurs are actually branchlets that are never going to develop; if they were stretched out, they would have individual needles.

Fruit. Oblong cones are 1 to 1½ inches long and sit erect on the branches. They are covered with a white fuzz, and long, pointed bracts extend out from under the scales.

Bark, Twigs. New twigs are somewhat fuzzy, but become smooth with age. The bark is a rusty red-orange, rather like the ponderosa pine.

The larches (also called tamarack) occupy an unusual position in the plant world: they are needle-leaf trees, conifers, which are also deciduous. In the fall, the trees are brilliant yellow splashes among the evergreens. Shorter days make the needles drop, but the trees retain a recognizable conifer shape (there's also the big pile of needles under the tree to help identify it!).

A mature Western larch will be 100 to 150 feet high and 3 to 4 feet in diameter; a tree 16 inches in diameter could be 500 years old. The largest living tree, in Montana, is 177 feet high and 7 feet 9 inches thick, with a spread of 27 feet. Larches are found at altitudes of 1000 to 5000 feet, and are usually mixed with evergreens, primarily lodgepole pine, Douglas fir, and Engelmann spruce. Occasionally, especially in Montana, they form pure stands. They grow best on north exposures, and seem to prefer rolling topography. They will tolerate an extreme range of temperature, from 118°F to -24°F, and they prefer a yearly rainfall of at least 28 inches.

Mature trees have a very thick bark (3 to 6 inches), which contains relatively little resin; this makes them very resistant to fire damage. Immature trees, however, with their thin bark, are vulnerable to fire, but the seeds re-establish quickly on burned-over land. Western larch and lodgepole pine are frequent competitors for the same space. If the pines get a head start, their shade will stunt the larch seedlings, which need full sun to survive. But if the larches become established first, they will outgrow the pines.

The wood of the Western larch is fine-grained, heavy, and durable. It is used frequently to make posts, mine timbers, and utility poles. Because of its denseness, larch wood makes a very fine, hot-burning fuel. But builders know they should never use it to make concrete forms, for it contains a certain sugar which reacts with concrete and prevents it from curing. A special gum which is commercially extracted from larch wood is used in printing, in pharmaceutical products, in paint, and in baking powder.

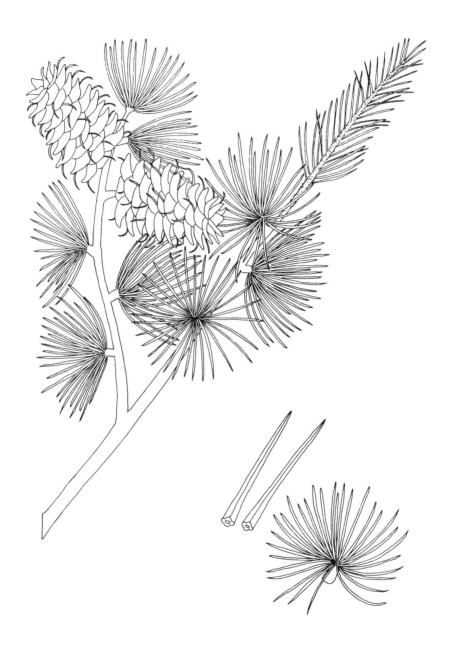

ALPINE LARCH
Larix lyallii
Lair-icks lye-*all*-ee

Key Identifiers. The seasonal color identifies it as a larch; soft, white wool on new twigs distinguishes it as the alpine species. See below for larch comparisons.

General Shape. A smallish tree, with a long, pointy crown, irregular and unsymmetrical. Trunks are often contorted, free of branches halfway up; branches of varying length, usually turning up at the ends. Even full-sized trees have the stunted look typical of many alpine plants.

Leaves. Soft, short needles, about 1 inch long, in bundles of 30 to 40. Shows the same seasonal color changes as the Western larch, but has one significant difference: in cross-section, the needles have 4 distinct sides.

Fruit. Small (1½ to 2 inches) cones, purplish-red, stand erect on the branches. Very stiff, purple bracts stick out from under the scales, which are covered with white woolly hair. Good cone crops are produced at irregular intervals.

Bark, Twigs. Bark of young trees is smooth and ashy gray; on older trees, reddish or purplish brown, lightly furrowed with loose scales; bark is quite thin. New-growth twigs are covered with a fine white woolly hair, which gives this tree the name of "woolly larch"—a clear characteristic of the species.

Alpine larch is a small tree, 30 to 40 feet high and 1 to 2 feet in diameter, and not heavily abundant. Largest living, 99 feet high, 56 feet across, 6 feet 3 inches thick, is in Chelan County, Washington. As you might assume from its common name, this is a high-elevation tree, normally found at or near timberline; but it does not form dense stands like subalpine fir and mountain hemlock. In this harsh climate, it often has a twisted appearance, but is an extremely tough tree. Its typical habitat is a rockpile. A tree 20 feet high can be bent to ground by snow and spring upright when thaw comes. Often lives 400 to 600 years.

Many trees are so severely stunted when grown in the cold climate of alpine zones that they seem more like shrubs than trees. However, alpine larch takes a recognizable tree form at timberline; invading alpine meadows, it thus forms a buffer, permitting other subalpine understory vegetation to ascend above timberline. In this protective shield of larches, you will often find plants that would normally only grow at lower elevations.

The wood of alpine larch is fine-grained, heavy, and very durable, but since the trees are not easy to get to, it has little commercial value.

TO DISTINGUISH BETWEEN OUR LARCHES	
Alpine	Found only at very high elevations. Relatively short tree. Needle 4-sided in cross section. White woolly new twigs.
Western	Found at lower elevations. Taller tree. 3-sided needle. No white wool on twigs.

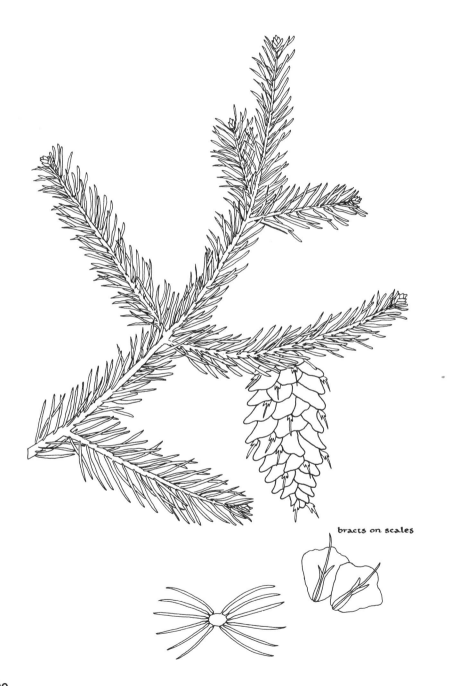

bracts on scales

100

DOUGLAS FIR
Pseudotsuga menziesii
Soo-dough-*soo*-gah men-*zeez*-eye

Key Identifier. Distinctive 3-pointed bracts between cone scales, and the sharp mahogany-colored tip at the branch ends.

General Shape. A broad, sharp pyramid atop a long straight trunk, which is clear of branches one-third to one-half its height. Branches are horizontal and tilt up at the ends; branchlets at the end of the limb have a characteristic downward slope that is somewhat like spread-out fingers. Immature trees have the shape of an old-fashioned Christmas tree: a full, graceful pyramid.

Leaves. Attached singly on all sides of the stem, not in a regular pattern. Needles are about 1 inch long, bright green above and paler below, with generally blunt tips. Basically flat in cross-section. Needles are attached to twig on a slender "stem" that leaves a raised leaf scar when pulled off the stem. When crushed, needles have a lemony smell.

Fruit. Cones are oval, cinnamon brown, 1½ to 4½ inches long, and hang down from branches. Scales are thin, stiff, and rounded. Unusual 3-pointed bracts, extending between scales, are a sure key to identification.

Bark. Generally dark red-brown on the surface, although color varies. Mature trees have very thick bark, as much as 10 inches near the bottom of the trunk, and very deep fissures. The terminal buds on all branches are shiny, mahogany-colored, and sharply pointed: another positive identifier.

Another example of the perversities of botanical naming: a Douglas fir is not a fir, nor is it a hemlock, even though *Pseudotsuga* means "false hemlock." It is a separate species unto itself. Douglas fir generally prefers mild, humid climates with dry summers. It is one of the most widespread conifers known, and occurs often in pure stands as well as in mixed forests. It's a long-lived, fast-growing tree: in its first 20 years, it grows 2 feet a year. Mature trees are usually 150 to 200 feet high and 3 to 6 feet in diameter, sometimes much larger. What is believed to be the largest recorded was 385 feet high. Largest now living is 221 feet high, 14½ feet in diameter, in Olympic National Park.

This tree is considered to be shade-tolerant, but less so than some of its common associates; therefore, it is not the surviving tree of an area, and pure stands are the result of clearcuts or fire.

The seeds are food to zillions of insects, to squirrels and chipmunks, who eagerly clip the cones before the seeds are even ripe.

Indian tribes found it a versatile tree. Bark was boiled into a dye; pitch was used on sores; pitch-tea served as a cold remedy. Boughs were used to make steam in sweathouses, and one Northwest tribe ceremoniously burned the cones to stop the rains.

This is one of the most important and valuable timber trees in the world, and is greatly sought for structural timber, plywood, paper, particleboard, and hundreds of other uses.

A SPECIAL NOTE ABOUT IDENTIFYING FIRS

It is fairly easy to know that a tree in question is a fir; if the question is, *which* fir, it isn't so easy. Botanists and foresters have been known to go quietly insane attempting to identify fir species. Two aspects of Mother Nature makes the problem especially difficult: The same species will take different forms in different parts of the West; and species of firs inter-breed, producing trees which have some characteristics of both, but are not definably either one.

The table below will give you the immediate clues that point to a true fir, and on the next page, a capsule of the characteristics that distinguish between the various firs of the region.

ALL FIRS HAVE THESE CHARACTERISTICS IN COMMON

- Narrow, pointed crown with primarily horizontal branches.

- Overall look of foliage is very regular, almost like a crewcut: needles curve up to the top and seem to be sheared off, all at the same height.

- Needles are attached singly, not in bundles.

- Needles do not have a perceptible "stem," but are attached directly to the branch.

- When needle is pulled off, it leaves a round, depressed scar on the stem.

- The cones sit up very straight on top of the branch, and are found in the highest branches of the tree.

- Cones do not fall off intact, but disintegrate slowly, losing a few scales at a time in the fall. In winter, you will see the leftover "spikes" of the cone core still on the branches.

- Young twigs have small blisters filled with resin; they can be burst open with your finger.

HOW TO DISTINGUISH BETWEEN OUR FIRS

Subalpine   Is found in subalpine zones. Needles dull, dark green with white lines on both surfaces. Needles all curve up toward top of stem. Cone is dark, purple, 2 to 4 inches long. Resin pockets deep into the bark. Usually a tall, thin shape like a church steeple.

Pacific
Silver   Needles are shiny, dark green on top, with silvery undersides. Needles on top of stem lean forward, toward the tip of branch. Buds at tip are perfectly round. Bark is smooth, much lighter gray than others, and has white patches. Cones purple.

White   Needles yellow-green with a white tinge. Needle arrangement is two-ranked, but scraggly. Needles up to 3 inches long, much longer than other firs. Cones olive green to brown.

Grand   Needles dark yellow-green above, with whitish undersides. Needle arrangement is two-ranked and extremely flat; they seem to have been ironed. Needles are two lengths, one twice as long as the other. Needle tips are notched. Cones light yellow-green. Grows at sea level.

Noble   Cones larger than other firs, completely covered with pointed bracts like shingles. Needles 4-angled in cross-section. Round crown. Hockey-stick needle.

SUBALPINE FIR
Abies lasiocarpa
Ay-beez *lass*-ee-oh-*kar*-pah

Key Identifier. At high elevations, its very thin, pointed crown, much like a church steeple. The only true fir with resin blisters deep within the grooves of its bark.

General Shape. At elevations of about 5000 feet, the tree develops a crown with an almost unbelievably sharp point; it has been compared to the Eiffel Tower in overall shape. When grown at timberline, it is often stunted to a low, gnarled ground-hugger called "Krumholz" form. Trees in the open often have limbs down to the ground. In dense stands 20 to 40 feet of the trunk will be bare.

Leaves. Needles are deep, dull blue-green, 1 to 1¾ inches long, flat in cross-section, and have a notch in the tip. They are attached all around the twig, but almost all curve upward toward the top, almost as if they have been combed. New-growth needles often have a silvery cast overlying the dark green.

Fruit. Cone is dark purple, cylindrical, 2 to 4 inches high. Scales are shaped like fans but longer than they are wide. Rounded bracts are hidden by the longer scales. When it is ripe, the cone does not simply fall off the tree, but gradually disintegrates, losing a few scales at a time, until nothing remains but the spiky "stem" of the cone.

Bark. Bark of young trees is thin and smooth, gray color with conspicuous resin blisters. Mature bark can be 1 to 1½ inches thick, very hard, with shallow furrows and rough red scales; resin blisters are tucked into the furrows.

Logically, subalpine fir grows where subalpine conditions predominate: a harsh cold, wet climate and thin, poor soils. Alone, at the highest elevations or exposed places, the "Krumholz" form is perpetuated by the weight of heavy snows which presses branches and trunk to the ground, where they root. Lower down, clumps of subalpine fir may exist as pioneer islands in alpine meadows. Lower still, it combines with Engelmann spruce and/or mountain hemlock, forming dense stands which are notable for the tangle of stumps, downed trees and branches caused by blowdown.

The seeds of this tree are very popular with small animals, for sources of food are scarce in subalpine areas.

This is the smallest of the true firs; at maturity it reaches a height of 65 to 100 feet, with a diameter of 14 to 24 inches.

Because its lower limbs persist on the tree, subalpine fir is particularly susceptible to fire. It suffers an even greater danger from a tiny European insect, the balsam woolly aphid, which has the potential of killing off all of this species, unless science soon finds a solution.

The wood of this tree is not of great commercial value, although it is often cut with Engelmann spruce and used for rough construction lumber.

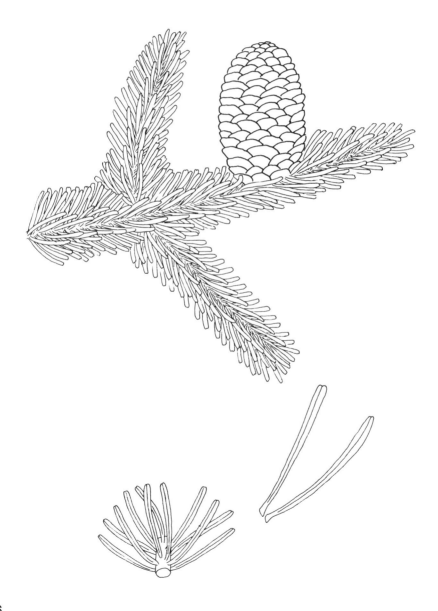

PACIFIC SILVER FIR
Abies amabilis
Ay-beez ah-*mob*-il-iss

Key Identifier. Distinctive bark is ghost-gray, with white splotches, and almost always smooth. Buds at tip of branches are round as a ball, and covered with resin.

General Shape. *Abies amabilis* in Latin means "lovely fir," and when you see it in the forest you will agree. It is a straight tree with a trunk which seems very slim for its height. It has a wide, conical crown of dense, heavily foliaged branches which grow almost down to the ground when the tree is found in the open. In the forest, the crown is also a wide cone but does not extend so far down the trunk.

Leaves. Needles are ¾ to 1¼ inches long, flat in cross-section, and have a groove at the top of the needle and a notch in the tip. Tops are dark, rich, shiny green; underneath, two bands of white give a shiny, silvery look to the underside of the foliage. Needles grow on all surfaces of the branch, but their growth pattern is such that they *appear* to be bunched at the top. Also, the needles on the top side tend to grow forward toward the outer end of the branch.

Fruit. Cone is dark purple, 3½ to 5 inches long, barrel-shaped and, like all true firs, stands erect on the branch. The scales are almost as wide as they are high, and the round bracts are shorter than the scales.

Bark, Twigs. Bark of the tree is one major key to its identification. It is thin and smooth, except on very old trees, and even then furrowed only at the base. Pale ashy gray, with conspicuous white patches. Twigs are stout, very slightly hairy, orange- or red-brown. The bud at the end of the twig is dark purple, shiny, resin-covered and completely round, ⅛ to ¼ inches in diameter.

Pacific silver fir prefers a maritime climate that is humid or semi-humid, with a warm growing season and cool winters, and can be found at elevations as high as 5000 feet. It is present in many common forest associations, usually with Western hemlock and mountain hemlock; these three form a distinct forest zone in the Cascades. Because it is shade-tolerant, this fir is able to survive in the shadow of bigger trees. Silver fir seeds germinate in damp ground and start growth faster than other conifers it occurs with.

The normal mature size is 150 to 180 feet high, and 3 to 5 feet in diameter; the national champion, in Olympic National Park, is 200 feet high and 6 feet 10 inches thick. The oldest known tree recorded, on Vancouver Island, B.C., was 540 years old.

Pacific silver fir has some commercial value as saw timber, used for construction materials, boxes and crates, planing mill products and general millwork. Commercial lumbermen often call this "white fir." The tree is occasionally used as a landscaping ornamental.

WHITE FIR
Abies concolor
Ay-beez *con*-color

Key Identifier. Needle arrangement is more or less two-ranked, but needles have a scraggly, irregular appearance. Needles much longer than other firs (up to 3 inches).

General Shape. Grown in the open, this is a formal, pyramidal tree, with extremely dense foliage, and covered to the ground with branches arranged loosely in tiers. The upper branches often are slightly ascending, with the lower ones slightly descending; the side branches form flat sprays. Because of their very regular shape, young trees are often used for Christmas trees.

Leaves. Needles are 2 to 3 inches long, green with a bluish cast, flat, and bluntly pointed. Both sides of the needle have a white tinge. Needles are attached in a manner that is basically two-ranked, but rather scraggly and uneven. Needles curve upward from bottom of the branch, up toward the top-side; on the lower branches, needles stand out horizontally, with less curve.

Fruit. Cones stand upright on the branches, are almost always found on the topmost part of the crown. They are 3¼ to 4¼ inches long, barrel-shaped, and of a color which changes from yellow-green when young to olive-green or brown to maturity. Bracts are hidden between scales.

Bark, Twigs. On mature trees, bark is an ashy color (whence cometh the common name), 4 to 6½ inches thick, extremely hard, and very rough and ridged. Younger bark is smooth and gray-brown. Tips of winter buds are round and covered with a resin that looks like dried sugar.

White fir, which is also known as balsam fir or silver fir, grows best in cool climates, and seems to prefer north-facing slopes. It is found at a wide range of elevations. Most mature trees reach a height of 140 to 160 feet, with a diameter of 40 to 60 inches. The largest living is 179 feet high, with a spread of 34 feet, and 8 feet 8 inches thick.

Concolor fir is a fairly abundant species, and grows both in pure stands and mixed forests. It is quite tolerant to shade, and so can become established in deep forests where other, larger trees already grow. In the southern Cascades and Siskiyous it forms pure stands above the mixed conifer zone. Its initial growth rate is slow, but accelerates greatly after 30 years, so that eventually it will shade out and overcome competing species.

Young trees are susceptible to fire damage and to breakage from the weight of snow on the limbs. Diseases open spiral cracks in the bark, which fill with water, then freeze, expand and cause an even larger crack; severe damage can result.

The wood of white fir makes an excellent saw timber and source of plywood. It is also a popular ornamental plant.

109

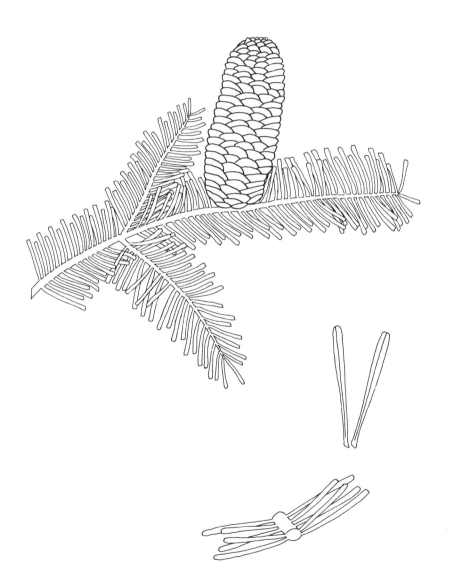

GRAND FIR
Abies grandis
A*y*-beez *grand*-iss

Key Identifier. In the lower part of the tree, the needles are arranged in two-ranked rows that are very regular and very flat, as if pressed in a book. Needles of two distinct lengths, one half as long as the other.

General Shape. When found in the open, the trunk is tall, straight and tapers very gradually, with branches almost to the ground. Tree often appears wider in the middle because of drooping branches. The top is pointed but widens quickly to a broad crown. Branches droop downward, then ends curve up. In a closed stand, the lower two-thirds of trunks are bare.

Leaves. Dark yellow-green needles are 1¼ to 2¼ inches long, with a groove along the top side and a distinct notch in the tip; the undersides show two strips of white. They are attached to the branch in a very flat plane, forming two flattened rows on opposite sides. Needles of two different lengths—one twice as long as the other—will be found on the same twig.

Fruit. Cone is 2 to 4¼ inches long, cylindrical, sits straight up on the branches, and is a characteristic light yellow-green color. Seeds may be dispersed by wind as much as 400 feet from the parent tree.

Bark, Twigs. Bark on young trees is gray-brown with large white patches and conspicuous resin blisters; older trees have bark 2 to 3 inches thick with hard, red-brown ridges. Growing bud is blunt, ⅛ to ¼ inches long, and usually covered with resin.

Grand fir is most frequently found in stream bottoms, valleys and mountain slopes in the Pacific Northwest, where rainfall is 20 to 50 inches per year. It occurs from sea level up to elevations of 5000 feet. It does not often form a pure stand, but is found in association with Douglas fir and Western larch.

Seedlings are easily damaged by burns from direct sunlight; this means that we seldom see a pure stand or single trees in the open, but more often find grand fir as understory plants in dense forests. The needles are very resistant to cold damage, but young trees are often broken by the weight of snow on the branches.

Grand firs usually reach a height of 125 to 150 feet with a 1 to 3-foot diameter; the largest living tree, in Mt. Rainier National Park, is 175 feet high and 7 feet thick.

This tree is susceptible to heart rot damage: a fungus enters the tree through dead lower limbs or from areas of physical damage. Seeds of grand fir feed many forest animals; as many as 25% of the seed crop in any year are eaten.

The wood of the grand fir is not especially important commercially but is sometimes cut for building material and pulpwood.

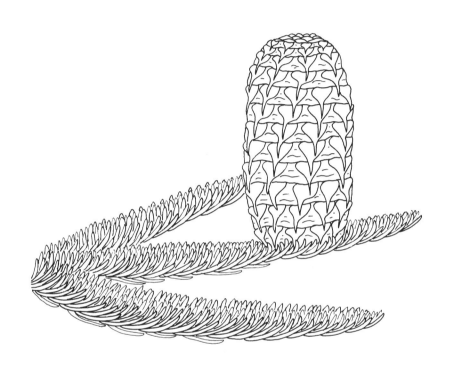

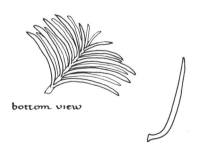

bottom view

NOBLE FIR
Abies procera
A*y*-beez *pross*-er-ah

Key Identifier. Large cones. Down-pointing bracts which almost completely cover cone. Needle shaped like a hockey stick. Round-top crown.

General Shape. A tall tree with a very straight trunk and a crown which is narrow and cone-shaped, but rounded at the top rather than pointy, like most firs. Branches are short, very stiff-looking, and stand out straight from the tree, except the oldest ones at the bottom, which tend to droop downward. Young trees have a sharp cone-shaped crown, with branches nearly to the ground.

Leaves. Needles are 1 to 1½ inches long, bright to dark bluish-green, and tinged with silver. Top of needles has a distinct groove, and tip is usually blunt. In the upper part of the tree, needles are four-sided; lower branches have flat needles, often with a notch in the tip. All needles curve up toward the top of the stem, and have a very regular, smooth appearance, as if someone had combed the needles upward, then given them a crewcut. Needle shape is very distinctive: the first ⅛ inch of the needle grows parallel to the stem, then it curves upward to the top of the branch. If you pull off a needle, you will see that it's an exact miniature of a hockey stick.

Fruits. Cone is unusually large for a fir (4 to 6 inches long), cylindrical in shape, and yellow-brown to purple. As with all firs, it sits erect on the branch. The cones of a noble fir have a look which is quite distinctive, and one way by which you can always know it (if you can find a cone). The bracts are long and pointed, and extend well beyond the scale tips. The extended part of the bract just covers the next lower scale, which gives the entire cone the look of being shingled. Seen at arm's length, the tips of the bracts are in such a regular pattern that they seem to spiral around the cone. A single mature tree may produce 500 cones a year, but its seeds do not usually germinate after their first year.

Bark, Twigs. Bark is very thin (about 1¼ inches), dark gray to gray-brown, and fairly smooth but broken into a small rectangular pattern of scales. When the scales flake off, they reveal a red-brown inner bark. The tip bud is covered with resin and with tiny rust-colored hair.

Noble fir grows best in very humid climates with a cool, short growing season; average annual rainfall must be high, but summer rainfall light. It is found at altitudes from 1500 to 4000 feet. It normally reaches a height of 100 to 150 feet, although a living specimen of 278 feet has been recorded.

This tree has few significant diseases but is very vulnerable to fire because of its thin bark. Intolerant of shade, it requires full sunlight to become established. In its first year, noble fir is a slow grower, increasing 1 foot in height every 3 or 4 years. At about 12 years, however, it suddenly speeds up, and eventually will overtake other trees in the area. It is thought to be the longest-lived fir, reaching 600 to 700 years.

The wood is relatively heavy and hard, and works easily. It is used mainly for boxes and crates. High-grade clear lumber is used for interior finish, moldings, siding, sash and door stock. Wooden venetian blinds were made almost exclusively of noble fir.

LODGEPOLE PINE / SHORE PINE
Pinus contorta
Pine-us con-*tort*-ah

Key Identifier. Two needles per bundle. Cones and needles much smaller than other pines.

General Shape. Species has two very distinct shapes, depending on locale. Near the coast, where it is called shore pine, tree is short (25 to 30 feet), with a dense round crown, the branches far down on an often twisted trunk. Inland, it is called lodgepole pine, a tall (50 to 100 feet) slender tree with a very straight trunk and a small crown of short branches high up in the tree.

Leaves. Short (1 to 3 inches), somewhat twisted needles in bundles of 2. Near the coast, needles are dark yellow-green; inland, a brighter green color.

Fruit. Egg-shaped yellow-brown cone, 1 to 2 inches long, often in clusters hanging down from the branch. Scales are thicker at the tips, usually armed with sharp spines.

Bark. Orange-brown to gray, and slightly scaly.

A *Pinus contorta* growing in the interior looks so entirely different from a *Pinus contorta* growing near the coast that you might easily think they were two different trees. In fact, botanists have argued for years over whether to consider them as two separate subspecies. It seems generally agreed now, however, that the two should be considered one.

This pine grows from sea level up to 11,000 feet, in many kinds of climatic environment, and is abundant throughout much of the West. It is the state tree of Wyoming.

The bark of lodgepole pine is very thin, and so the tree is quite susceptible to fire damage. In a sense, Nature has compensated for this by developing a unique cone. The lodgepole cone often remains on the tree for years after maturing, its scales tightly closed. They will open only when exposed to heat, and so a forest fire which destroys the trees of an area also opens the way for seeding of lodgepole, which then becomes the first tree species to fill in a burned-over area. The trees are slow-growing, but long-lived.

The contorted and strangely beautiful trees that we see in both wet and dry sites along the Pacific Coast are usually *Pinus contorta;* they serve a valuable function in stabilizing the fragile dunes. The mountain tree is called "lodgepole" because it was so frequently used by the Indians as the framing structure for their teepees or lodges. These tall, superbly straight trees often lasted a family for a lifetime. The tree also provided medicine; pitch was placed on open sores, and the buds were chewed as a balm for sore throat.

Today, lodgepole pine is an important timber species, providing lumber, pulpwood, poles, posts, and mine timbers.

PONDEROSA PINE
Pinus ponderosa
Pie-nus pon-der-*oh*-sa

Key Identifier. Exceptionally long needles, and lustrous orange bark with round-edged flakes like pieces of a jigsaw puzzle. This is a 3-needle pine.

General Shape. Most often, shows a long, narrow crown, with scattered branches that turn at up the ends. Single trees growing in the open may have branches all down the trunk; in groups, the trunks will be clear 40 to 50 feet up, except for a very unusual quirk: many trees have a single live branch far down on the trunk, perhaps 20 feet below the base of the crown.

Leaves. Dark yellow-green needles up to 10 inches long, occur almost always in bunches of 3; very occasionally in 2's; and sometimes in 4's and 5's on young trees. Needles are densely grouped at the ends of branches, giving the effect of a brush. They fall from the tree after 3 years.

Fruit. With a characteristic egg shape, cones are 3 to 6 inches long and pendent. Scales are thick at the tip and have a sharp spine. Mature trees can have as many as 200 cones at a time. When the cones fall from the tree, part of the bottom of the cone remains on the branch, leaving a rosette of scales on display.

Bark, Twigs, Root. On younger trees, the bark is an undistinguished brownish black; older trees develop a thick spongy bark, in flat scales with irregular shapes very much like the pieces of a jigsaw puzzle. As the trees mature, the bark color changes to a distinctive rusty orange color; in late afternoon sunset, it fairly glows. New-growth twigs smell like oranges when they are broken. A long taproot makes for a very stable tree, which stands up well to strong winds.

The ponderosa is the most wide-ranging pine in North America; it is found in all eleven of our Western states. It grows best in hot climates with rainfall from 18 to 43 inches a year. It is found in association with almost all our native forest plants, from sea level to altitudes of up to 9000 feet in the southern parts of its range. A tall, regal tree, it is usually about 100 feet high and 3 feet in diameter when mature. The largest living is 223 feet high, 68 feet across, 7 feet thick, near Plumas, California.

Because of very thick bark (3 to 4 inches), mature ponderosas are very resistant to fire damage, but they are vulnerable to the many species of pine beetle. The seeds are an important food source to all the seed-eaters in the forest. Albert squirrels are largely dependent upon ponderosa pine for food. Seed caches left by ground squirrels probably contribute to the regeneration of ponderosa pine forests.

Look around you. The forest is probably very dry looking, with a smooth-swept forest floor. Ponderosa pine will thrive at drier sites than any other midelevation tree, except junipers. The lack of rainfall and passage of fires keeps the understory thin and parklike. These large pines often grow on level or lightly rolling ground, where melting winter snows do not run off but sink to the subsoil, where deep taproots pick it up.

The state tree of Montana, ponderosa pine is a significant commercial timber tree, used principally in furniture, plywood, fiberboard, and paper. "Knotty pine" paneling is usually made from ponderosa wood.

SUGAR PINE
Pinus lambertiana
Pie-nus *lam*-ber-ti-*anna*

Key Identifier. King-size cones, more than a foot long. This is a 5-needle pine. See page 125 for pine comparisons.

General Shape. A tall, straight tree with a wide, flat crown, and comparatively few branches. The branches stand out from the trunk at a 90-degree angle.

Leaves. Needles appear in bunches of five, are 3 to 4 inches long and deep bluish-green, and have 3 sides. They have long, fine white lines on all 3 surfaces, and are frequently twisted.

Fruit. Largest cones are 12 to 24 inches long and 2½ to 3½ inches in diameter. Cones are flexible and have no spines on the scales. Seeds are about the size of a kernel of corn, and have one wing, 1 to 2 inches long, which doesn't work very well—the seeds almost thump to the forest floor.

Bark. Reddish brown and formed in long plates, somewhat like the ponderosa pine.

The common name of this tree comes from the sugary-tasting resin which exudes from tree wounds; it was eaten as a snack by early Indians. It really is sweet but taste only a little—it acts as a laxative! Sugar pines are found at elevations ranging from 1700 feet at the north limit of their range to 10,000 feet at the south end. They prefer humid areas, with rainfall of about 50 inches a year, and are most commonly found on north- and east-facing slopes. They do not normally form pure stands, but are mixed with yellow pine, Douglas fir, and incense cedar.

The tree which produces such a large cone must itself be of magnificent size; the sugar pine regularly reaches a height of 160 to 180 feet. This makes it the tallest pine on our continent; only the redwood, giant sequoia and the Douglas fir are larger. The trunk is unusually straight and free of branches, which made sugar pine the favorite building material of early settlers in the Sierra foothills. John Sutter's mill in California, where gold was later discovered, was set up to cut sugar pine.

The large seeds are edible (they were a popular food for West Coast Indians), but you'll have to move fast to beat the squirrels and woodpeckers. Douglas pine squirrels eat about half the seed crop before they even mature, and the whiteheaded woodpecker (who is really looking for the sugar pine beetle) ruins another third. With all these hazards, sugar pine doesn't invade adjacent sites very quickly.

Few diseases trouble the sugar pine, but young trees are especially vulnerable to fire. The sugar pine is a major commercial timber tree, widely used in construction lumber: one large tree can yield 25,000 board-feet! The fine-grained wood is excellent for door, sashes, moldings, and boat decks. It is one of the few trees that can be used for pipes in church organs.

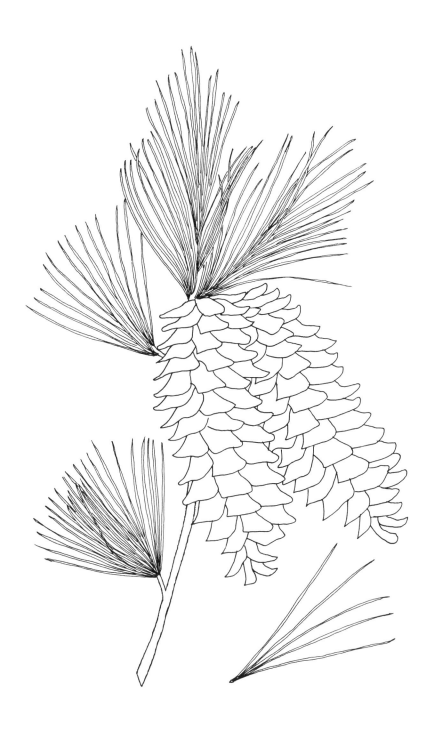

WESTERN WHITE PINE
Pinus monticola
Pie-nus *mon*-ti-*coh*-la

Key Identifier. An unusual growth habit: in the open, these trees have one, or several, thick horizontal branches which stick out 10 to 15 feet beyond the other, more slender, drooping branches. This is a 5-needle pine. It has many similarities to the sugar pine, but there are clear differences in cone and bark; see chart on page 125.

General Shape. Usually tall and thick, with a very symmetrical crown of quite short, slender branches that droop downward.

Leaves. Rigid needles, 2 to 5 inches long, are in bunches of 5. Color is blue-green, slightly tinged with white.

Fruit. Cones are slender, slightly curving, 4 to 10 inches long (smaller than sugar pine). They hang down from branches on long stalks, and never appear on trees that are less than 30 to 40 feet high. Compared to other pines, this one has relatively few cones.

Bark. On mature trees, the gray bark is broken into small squares, making a pattern like old-fashioned floor tiles; this is very characteristic of the tree. Young trees have quite smooth bark.

The Western white pine likes a cool, dry climate, and is usually found in mountainous areas, from 2500 to 6000 feet but occasionally at sea level. It is most abundant in the northern Rockies. It does not usually grow in pure stands, but in association with many common evergreens. Trees are about 100 feet high at maturity, with a 3-foot diameter. Largest Western white pine is 239 feet high, 40 feet across, 6½ feet thick, near Medford, Oregon.

A serious hazard is the white pine blister rust, a fungus disease that will kill the tree if it takes hold. The disease appears only where currant and gooseberry shrubs grow, as these bushes harbor the fungus during one phase of its life cycle.

Western white pine, which is the state tree of Idaho, provided food for Indians, who boiled its bark to make a healing tea for stomach disorders and tuberculosis. Pulverized bark made a poultice for cuts and sores.

This is an important timber tree; its wood is lightweight, close-grained, fairly durable, very uniform in texture. It seasons without warping, saws easily, takes nails without splitting. It is often used in window and door frames, cabinetwork, indoor paneling, and it is the preferred wood for wooden matches.

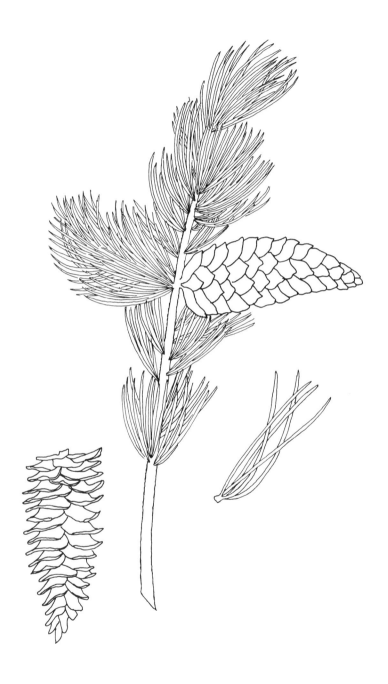

Key Identifier. Branches are so limber you could tie one into a knot; very thick tips on cone scales. This is a 5-needle pine. See pine comparison chart, page 125.

General Shape. Short, thick trunk with an irregular crown. On high, exposed slopes, the trees show a stunted, twisted form, very low to the ground.

Leaves. Needles are 1½ to 3 inches long, dark green or deep yellow-green, and in bunches of 5. The bundles are clustered in dense masses toward the end of the branches. Needles drop off after 5 years, approximately.

Fruit. Cone is cylindrical, yellowish brown, 3 to 8 inches long, and hangs down from the branch. The tips of the scales are rounded, and very thick, but do not have spines. The seeds, comparatively large and without wings, are favorites of birds and squirrels.

Bark, Twigs. New-growth twigs are smooth, light gray; on older branches, the bark is thickened, and dark brown, with deep furrows.

Limber pine, a very durable tree, grows at or near timberline, from 5000 to 9000 feet. It seems to grow best on east slopes, and does not usually form a stand, but grows in association with white fir, hemlock, lodgepole pine, Douglas fir, and Engelmann spruce.

Compared to some forest species, this is a small tree, usually 25 to 30 feet with 12 to 30 inches diameter. The largest living is in Little Willow Canyon, Utah; 43 feet high, 36 feet across, and 9 feet 4 inches thick. Because of its size, and attractive appearance, it is commonly used as an ornamental landscape tree.

The heartwood of the limber pine is dense, seasons well, and works easily, but does not last well. This, combined with its inaccessibility, makes the limber pine of little commercial significance.

Limber pine, like other subalpine species, is very durable, but this one is even more so than most, as it is found most often in the drier, more windswept parts of the treeline zone. Scattered among other subalpine associates, it fares poorly, producing skimpy specimens. Whenever the habitat becomes too harsh for other species, limber pine forms distinctive stands of a few trees. These have a skimpy, upper crown and abundant large upward-reaching branches in the lower crown.

WHITEBARK PINE
Pinus albicaulis
Pie-nus al-bi-*call*-us

Key Identifier. The chalky white bark on young trees. This is a 5-needle spine. In many ways, it closely resembles the limber pine (page 123); but there are distinct differences in cones. See species comparison chart below.

General Shape. Normally a long, twisted trunk, with long branches far down the trunk. Crown is broad and spreading, but irregular, with dead branches dangling down. On windy slopes, it will be stunted into a low shrub with branches spreading far across the ground.

Leaves. Dark yellow-green needles are 1½ to 3 inches long, stiff, and slightly curved. Needles in bunches of 5, clustered down toward the end of the branch, remain on the tree 7 to 8 years.

Fruit. The pendulous cone is 1½ to 3 inches long (smaller than the limber pine) and deep red to purplish brown; the scales are thick and often sharp-pointed. Cones fall to the ground unopened, and the wingless seeds are released only when the cone disintegrates; in the cold, dry atmosphere at timberline, this can take several years.

Bark, Twigs. Bark on young trees is thin, smooth and chalkwhite; on older trees, it becomes brownish-white, about ½ inch thick, and is broken into narrow platey scales. New-growth twigs are hairy; buds are sharp-pointed.

Like the limber pine, this is a characteristic timberline species, especially in the Rockies. The whitebark pine survives extreme cold and intense winds. The branches are quite flexible, especially near the trunk; in high wind, they will bend rather than break. Whitebark pine is a slow grower, and make take 200 years to reach maturity. Its mature size varies from a low shrub, on wind-blasted slopes, to 50 feet; largest living is 85 feet high, 60 feet across, 6 feet thick, in Grand Teton National Park. Often pure stands.

Whitebark pine enjoys a curious relationship with a seed-eating bird, Clark's nutcracker. Seed dissemination is greatly the result of the efforts of this bird, which eats a few seeds, then hoards away the rest. New trees spring from forgotten hoards. This process may be the means whereby whitebark pine invades alpine meadows, establishes small clumps of trees which in turn become shelter for successive types of vegetation.

TO DISTINGUISH BETWEEN 5-NEEDLE PINES

These are two similar, both with bluish-green needles:

Sugar	Gigantic cones, red-brown bark in long plates.
Western white	Smaller cones than sugar. Gray bark in small squares like tiles.

These two are similar, both with yellow-green needles:

Limber	Cone is more than 3 inches long, yellow-brown; scales do not have sharp, spiny tips.
Whitebark	Cones 3 inches or shorter, deep red to purple, with sharp-pointed scales.

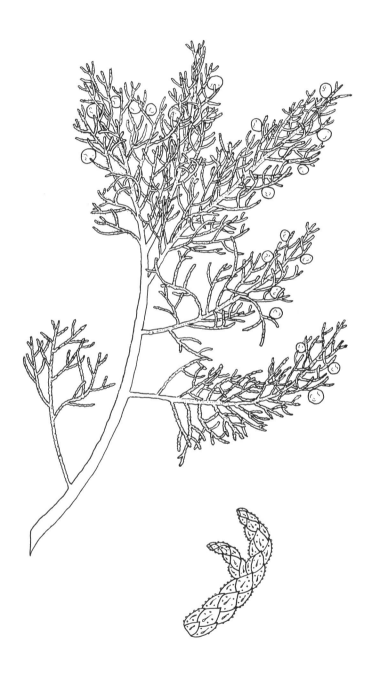

WESTERN JUNIPER
Juniperus occidentalis
June-*ip*-er-us oxy-din-*tal*-iss

Key Identifier. Dark blue berrylike cones, and one protruding dot of white resin on each scalelike leaf. See species comparison chart, page 129, and page 138.

General Shape. As a young tree, it is usually well-formed, but as it grows older, becomes irregular and ragged looking, with gnarled trunk and heavy limbs, forming a rather blunt top. Unlike most other Western trees, it doesn't have a standard silhouette, but is formed by the variables of its environment.

Leaves. Extremely small, scalelike leaves (⅟₁₆ to ⅛ inch) are quite flat and lie close to the branch, in staggered whorls of 3. If you look closely at a stem, you see the leaves forming six rows down the branch. Every leaf has a tiny white crumb of resin on the outer surface, which gives the foliage a rich and distinctive aroma.

Fruit. The blue-black fruit, which looks like a berry (indeed, it's about the size and color of a blueberry), is really a cone containing 2 to 3 seeds. Cone is covered with a white powdery bloom which you can rub off with your fingers. "Berries" are profuse, and hang on tree all winter. The fruit reminds many people of the aroma of gin. . .for a good reason: juniper berries are the prime flavoring of gin.

Bark, Twigs. Bark on young branches is a grayish tan which flakes off in square paperlike pieces, revealing a reddish undercolor. Older branches and trunk have thicker bark, up to 1½ inches, which is bright cinnamon color, stringy, and distinctly cut by wide, shallow grooves which are connected by diagonal furrows. Twigs are round.

Junipers as a group grow in the driest climates and the poorest soils. Western juniper inhabits the most arid regions of the Northwest states, where it is usually the only tree for miles around, in a land populated by range cattle, sagebrush and jackrabbits. Here the summers are hot and dry (less than 10 inches of rain per year) and winters are bitterly cold. The elevation may vary from sea level to 10,000 feet.

In such a narsn environment, Western juniper does not attain great size. A mature tree is usually 15 to 30 feet high with a diameter of 20 to 48 inches, and may be 200 to 300 years old. The largest living tree, in the Stanislaus National Forest, is 87 feet high and 13½ feet thick—strong testimony to the stubborn endurance of this tree.

The tree is found over a widespread range, but is nowhere very abundant, and usually occurs as a scattered woodland. It is completely unable to live in shade, and therefore does not compete with other species. It frequently invades grasslands that have been overgrazed, where there is no competition for the direct sunlight it requires. Seeds are commonly spread by birds that eat the berries; old fencerows are lined with junipers.

Juniper wood is fine-textured, easy to work, and amazingly durable; it has been the mainstay of generations of farmers and ranchers as a source of fenceposts.

128

ROCKY MOUNTAIN JUNIPER
Juniperus scopulorum
June-*ip*-er-us scop-you-*lore*-um

Key Identifier. Typical juniper "berries," but no resin dots on foliage. See chart below for comparison of juniper species; also see page 138.

General Shape. In an open, exposed setting, the tree often has the general appearance of a shrub: several trunks, and a low height, 15 to 20 feet. In sheltered areas, the tree is likely to have a single, straight trunk, up to 18 inches thick, and a slender pointed crown with drooping branches; total height may be 25 to 30 feet.

Leaves. Tiny, pointed scalelike leaves in two pairs of opposite rows, creating 4 columns of leaves marching down the stems. Leaves do not bear the small dot of resin that is found on Western juniper.

Fruit. A blue-black cone, containing 2 seeds, is much like a berry in appearance. Cones are covered with a white waxy bloom which makes the color seem bluer.

Bark, Twigs. Bark is gray-brown to somewhat reddish, thin, and divided by furrows into flat, interlacing ridges. Because of the 4-column arrangement of leaves, the twigs appear square and flat-sided.

Rocky Mountain juniper, like its more westerly counterpart, grows in areas that are very dry, very hot (in summer), very cold (in winter), with very poor, rocky, rather alkaline soil. . .harsh lands where it would seem no living thing could survive. In such country, the rugged juniper grows slowly, and never reaches large heights: in 80 years, it may be only 18 feet high. The same tough nature makes this a very long-lived tree; 300 years is common, and there is even a report of a 3000-year-old tree in Logan Canyon, Utah.

The trees cover a wide geographic range, but nowhere in that range are they found in great numbers; they mostly occur as single trees or small groups. They provide food for many birds, in particular the cedar waxwing, and the birds in turn disseminate the seeds.

In the Puget Sound area of Washington (where generally rainfall is high and climate is damp), there is a small microclimate that is more arid and therefore hospitable to the junipers, and here some Rocky Mountain juniper have been found. In this specialized zone, local Indians felt the tree had special properties, and they boiled its roots into a medicinal bath water for rheumatism; boiling juniper branches indoors was thought to disinfect the house.

TO DISTINGUISH BETWEEN JUNIPERS	
Western	Dots of white resin on back side of each leaf. Leaves arranged in 6 rows, making the twigs appear round. Bark is bright cinnamon color. Crown top rather blunt.
Rocky Mountain	No resin dots on leaves. Leaves arranged in 4 rows, giving the twigs a square look. Bark is gray-brown. Crown top rather pointed.

YELLOW CEDAR
Chamaecyparis nootkatensis
cam-i-*sip*-ah-riss *noot*-ka-*ten*-sis

Key Identifier. No white X's on bottom of leaves. Rough, shaggy bark. Rough texture of foliage. See comparisons on page 138.

General Shape. A medium-sized tree with drooping branches; foliage hangs down limply from branches, giving the tree a wilted appearance. Tip of leader is limp and droops over. Trees growing in the open may have branches down to the ground, while those in close stands will have limbs only in the top half. On large trees, the base of the trunk is not symmetrically round but is fluted. Trunk, which is not usually straight, rises in a sharp taper. The crown of the tree is the shape of a narrow cone, except on high, exposed ridges, where it may be a shaggy, sprawling shrub.

Leaves. Scalelike foliage is yellow-green arranged in two sets of alternate pairs, but without the white X's found on the reverse side of Port Orford cedar. Tips of scales are sharp-pointed and not flat to the branch, but attached more loosely, which gives the foliage a rough prickly texture. Like other Western cedars, branchlets of foliage are broad, flat sprays.

Fruit. Cone is small (¼ to ½ inch), round, reddish-brown. It has 2 to 4 scales with a sharp, straight point in the middle. Two winged seeds lie underneath each scale.

Bark. Bark is thin, gray-brown, deeply ridged and shaggy, and made up of long thin scales which are loose at each end.

The yellow cedar (also known as Alaska cedar and yellow cypress) grows very slowly where the climate is cool and humid; it is abundant in stream bottoms, basins, valleys, and moist slopes. Occasionally it forms a pure stand (especially in Alaska), but more commonly is found growing singly or in small clumps.

Usually this tree grows to a height of 80 to 100 feet, and 2 to 3 feet thick. The largest living specimen, in Washington, is 133 feet high and 9 feet 10 inches thick. This is a slow-growing tree, but a very long-lived one, and has been known to reach 3500 years.

Yellow cedar is relatively free of disease, but can be seriously damaged by fire, for its thin bark offers little defense. The flexible, drooping leader sheds snow from the top of the tree, causing the snow on lower branches to avalanche, thus minimizing damage from snow-weight.

Alaskan Indians prized the wood of yellow cedar for canoe paddles. Today it is valued for its high resistance to decay, and is used for poles, posts, pilings, and boat construction. The wood finishes beautifully and turns a characteristic bright yellow when wet. Varieties have been developed as landscape plants.

132

WESTERN RED CEDAR
Thuja plicata
Thoo-yah ply-*cate*-ah

Key Identifier. The cones sit erect on the top of branches, but lean backward toward the trunk of the tree. See comparisons, page 138.

General Shape. When young, or when grown in the open, this is a well-tapered pyramid-shaped tree, with straight trunk and branches nearly to the ground. Mature trees become very large, up to 200 feet high, with a blunt crown. This tree frequently develops two main leaders, giving the crown an especially dense look at the top. Branches curve downward, then turn up at the ends; sprays of foliage hang down from the branches like fringe. The trunks of mature trees are often twisted, and develop an extremely wide base that is deeply fluted.

Leaves. Scalelike leaves grow in two pairs, on alternate sides of the twigs. They are ⅛ to ¼ inch long, shiny, yellow-green. Foliage branchlets in a pattern of broad, flattened sprays with a smooth texture.

Fruit. Cone is small (½ inch), narrow oval-shaped, light russet brown, and clusters near the end of the branch. It sits on top of the branch, bent backward toward the main trunk. Cone has 4 to 6 pairs of thin, spiny scales, and produces 6 seeds per cone. Seeds are so small that forest animals overlook them, therefore lots of seeds survive for germination.

Bark. Bark of Western red cedar is a cinnamon color, on which the older parts have sometimes been weathered to a gray-brown. Distinct long seams create vertical ridges in bark surface. Bark has long fibrous stands that can be pulled away but which make the inner bark particularly strong. With care, a strand 20 to 30 inches long may be removed intact.

Western red cedar normally reaches a height of 150 to 200 feet in the best growing conditions: areas of abundant precipitation and high humidity. Tree will tolerate long, cold winters, but does best in areas of moderate temperature. It is generally found on stream bottoms, moist flats, and gentle lower slopes; and seems to favor the cooler, moister north slopes. Western red cedar can withstand dry climates if it has adequate soil moisture. It is found up to 5000 feet, occasionally as high as 7000 feet, but seldom grows in pure stands.

Because it grows most heavily in damp areas, this tree does not normally develop the long tap root needed by trees searching for water; thus a high wind can easily topple a large tree, even more so when the soil is shallow and moist. It is also very susceptible to fire damage because of its thin bark.

Western red cedar, a very important lumber tree today, was also important to Western Indians, who used it in construction of shelter, tools, and canoes; woven bark became clothing, art objects, and religious implements.

134

PORT ORFORD CEDAR
Chamaecyparis lawsoniana
Cam-i-*sip*-ah-riss *law-son*-ee-an̄na

Key Identifier. White X's on underside of scale leaves. See comparisons, page 138.

General Shape. A spirelike tree with wide-spreading branches, which on young trees turn upward but with age become characteristically horizontal. The trunk often has one or two bends.

Leaves. Small scalelike leaves in four rows down the stem, in opposite pairs. The scales overlap in such a way that the edges form white X's on the underside of the stem. Leaves are soft to the touch, shiny, dark green. Points of the leaf tips are short and blunt. Branchlets are flat sprays of foliage, all in one plane.

Fruit. Cone is small, ¼ in diameter, round and berrylike; even when the scales open, it maintains its round shape. Cones cluster on the underside of the branch. There are 8 to 10 scales, wedge-shaped, with a point in the center of the scale which curves over. The cone ripens in one season, and produces 2 to 4 seeds per scale. The seeds are relatively heavy and the short wings do not carry them far from the parent tree. Many seeds may lie dormant as much as 5 years before germinating.

Bark. On mature trees, bark is thick at base, 6 to 8 inches, and becomes thinner higher up. Bark is fibrous and stringy, weathered gray on the exterior and red-brown beneath. Deep, narrow vertical seams are characteristic.

Port Orford cedars grow in sea-facing slopes of the Oregon coast range and the Siskiyou Mountains, where the climate is characterized by wet winters, dry summers, uniform temperatures, and summer fog.

They normally reach a height of 140 to 180 feet; with a diameter of 4 to 6 feet. The largest living tree is 219 feet high and almost 12 feet thick.

Because the tree has no need to develop a long taproot, it is subject to severe windthrow, especially if heavy with snow. Young trees, with their thin bark, are susceptible to fire. Old trees develop a thick bark and are quite resistant to fire.

Few insects prey on this tree, but it has been greatly imperiled in recent years by a strain of root rot that is almost impossible to cure once established.

The wood of this tree is highly prized for fine wood products and furniture. It is considered the best wood for arrow shafts. In fact, arrow-making businesses in Coos County, Oregon, are noted for the high quality of their products. Because it is exceptionally durable, this cedar is used for sash and door construction, flooring, interior finish and in boat-building.

Several varieties of Port Orford cedar (called Lawson cypress by gardeners and landscape architects) have been horticulturally developed as nursery plants and are extremely popular for home landscaping.

INCENSE CEDAR
Libocedrus decurrens
Lie-boh-*see*-drus dee-*cur*-ens

Key Identifier. Most unusual cones, shaped like a clam shell hinged on the short side. Scalelike leaves much longer than they are wide. See comparisons on page 138.

General Shape. A fairly tall tree with a trunk which is quite wide at the base but tapers rapidly; branches are generally horizontal, with an upward turn at the ends. Young trees show a pointed cone-shaped crown; as it becomes older, the tree develops a rounded crown.

Leaves. Scalelike foliage arranged in sets of 4, closely overlapping each other. Unlike other cedars, the scales are much longer than they are wide (up to ½ inch long). Leaves are dark green, lustrous, and attached flat along the stem, with only the tip being loose. When they are crushed, leaves give off a spicy fragrance. Branchlets are set on stems in one flat plane. Leaves are shed in the second or third year, and also the twigs on which they are attached.

Fruit. Highly unusual cones hang downward from the very tips of the branches. They are ¼ to ½ inch long, red-brown, oblong, and look remarkably like a duck's bill or a clam shell hinged on the end. They open to reveal a slightly longer mid-scale, and then free four large winged seeds, which may be blown considerable distances.

Bark, Roots. Bark is thin, cinnamon red, furrowed, and peels into long fibrous strips. Wide lateral root system makes tree very firm in high winds.

Incense cedar grows in areas where the summer is dry and the annual rainfall is 20 to 80 inches. It will tolerate extremes of temperature from -30°F to 110°F and is found up to 7000 feet elevations, most often on west-facing slopes. The tree does not usually form pure stands, and usually comprises less than 30% of any stand.

Seedlings of incense cedar are extremely slow growers, and may take 3 to 5 years to reach a height of 6 inches. Because of this slow growth, incense cedar trees may form an understory to much younger, taller Douglas fir. This is a dry-country cedar. It is resistant to drought and other water shortages and thus thrives on south-facing slopes and dry sites. The largest living tree is 152 feet high and 12 feet 3 inches thick.

Mature incense cedars are likely to be the most seriously diseased of any tree in the area. The greatest damage is a fungus that enters the tree through fire scars, knots, and mechanical damage, and leaves pockets of powdery rot buried in the heartwood. It is also easily damaged by smog. This is the cedar tree whose wood is made into moth-proof chests. The tree is also the source of an oil used in making perfume, and supplies more than three-fourths of the wood for all the world's pencils.

A WORD ABOUT JUNIPERS AND CEDARS

The Cypress family includes trees and shrubs with scalelike leaves; our Western plants represent 4 genera from this family: *Libocedrus, Thuja, Chamaecyparis,* and *Juniperus.* The first three are commonly called cedars, but actually here in the West we do not have any native cedars. The true cedars belongs to the genus *Cedrus,* and are native to the Himalayas and the Mediterranean areas (the famed Cedars of Lebanon are true cedars). The trees that we call cedars are cousins, botanically speaking, and have many characteristics in common with each other and with the junipers.

To tell the difference between junipers and the other cousins, look to the fruit.

IS IT A CEDAR OR A JUNIPER?

Cedars　　　　The fruit is a woody cone. Trees grow to a large size in moist or cool areas.

Junipers　　　The fruit is like a berry. Tree form, which grows in warm, dry areas, is highly variable in shape. At high elevations, plant takes a shrubby form.

WHICH CEDAR DO I HAVE?

Cones are your first clue.

Incense cedar　　Elongated "duck bill" shaped cone.

Western red cedar　　Narrow oval cones, with dry scales, pointing back toward trunk.

Chamaecyparis (2 species)　　Small, round cones, with fleshy scales.

Then, to distinguish between the two *Chamaecyparises,* check the *foliage* and the points on the cone *scales.*

Port Orford cedar　　Bottom of leaves shows a pattern of white X's. Foliage is soft to the touch. The point in the center of the cone scales curves over.

Yellow cedar　　No white X's. Foliage rough and prickly. Scale points stick straight out.

Bibliography

Good Resources to Know About

Beyond the Aspen Grove. By A. Zwinger. Random House, 1970.

Covers the Rocky Mountain region. Written for the popular audience; well-illustrated.

Flora of the Pacific Northwest. By C. Leo Hitchcock and Arthur Cronquist. University of Washington Press, 1973.

A formal dichotomous key, covering trees, shrubs, and small plants of the Northwest area. A one-volume summary of a five-volume epic. Trained botanists consider this the last word in technical precision. For most of us, it's too intimidating to use. A large, heavy book, best used in the library.

Forest Trees of the Pacific Slope. By George B. Sudworth. Dover Books, 1967.

A reissue of a classic work (1908) by an energetic and respected Forest Service botanist. Excellent illustrations and meticulous descriptions of the trees, all the more significant because so much of Sudworth's research and writing is the basis of our present knowledge.

A Natural History of Western Trees. By Donald Culross Peattie. Houghton Mifflin Company, 1953.

> Covers all of Western North America. Botanical data is secondary to Peattie's colorful essays on the lyric nature and personality of the trees. Use a library copy; it's hefty.

Pacific Coast Tree Finder. By Tom Watts. Nature Study Guide, 1973.

> A pocket-sized manual, organized as a dichotomous key, but not overwhelming. A good tool if you want to learn how a key works.

Rocky Mountain Flora. By William A. Weber. University of Colorado Press, 1967.

> A recognized authority on identification of plants of the Rockies.

Rocky Mountain Trees. By Richard J. Preston, Jr. Dover Books, 1968.

> An updated reprint of a 1947 work. Handy and well-illustrated.

Silvics of Forest Trees of the United States. Agriculture Handbook No. 271. Forest Service, U.S. Dept. of Agriculture, 1965.

> Somewhat technical in tone, and a bit formidable in format, but nonetheless full of relevant information. Covers the entire U.S., but deals only with trees which have commercial value.

Trees of North America. By C. Frank Brockman. Golden Press, 1968.

> Covers all of North America; includes all native plants plus a few familiar species which have been introduced into our landscape. Succinct descriptions present the essential botanical data; color illustrations are excellent. Convenient paperback size. An all-around good buy.

Trees to Know in Oregon. By Charles R. Ross. Oregon State University Extension Service, Bulletin 697, reprinted 1972.

> A delightful book. A bit too wide for most pockets, but light and worth taking along. Interesting and important information, presented in simple, easy-to-understand style. Highly recommended.

Wildlife and Plants of the Cascades. By Charles Yocom and Vinson Brown. Naturegraph Publishers, 1971.

> As the title says, covers only the trees of the Cascade region. Describes the various forest zones as plant communities, then cross-references the plants and the wildlife likely to be found in each zone. Once you get the rhythm of how it is organized, this is a good book for understanding the interrelatedness of plants and animals in the forests.

ᵀIndex

141

get
FALCON GUIDED

 are available for where-to-go hiking, mountain biking, rock climbing, walking, scenic driving, fishing, rockhounding, paddling, birding, wildlife viewing, and camping. We also have FalconGuides on essential outdoor skills and subjects and field identification. The following titles are currently available, but this list grows every year. For a free catalog with a complete list of titles, call FALCON toll-free at 1-800-582-2665.

BIRDING GUIDES
Birding Arizona
Birding Minnesota
Birder's Guide to Montana
Birding Texas
Birding Utah

FIELD GUIDES
Bitterroot: Montana State Flower
Canyon Country Wildflowers
Great Lakes Berry Book
New England Berry Book
Plants of Arizona
Rare Plants of Colorado
Rocky Mountain Berry Book
Southern Rocky Mtn. Wildflowers
Tallgrass Prairie Wildflowers
Western Trees
Wildflowers of Southwestern Utah
Willow Bark and Rosehips

FISHING GUIDES
Fishing Alaska
Fishing the Beartooths
Fishing Florida
Fishing Maine
Fishing Michigan
Fishing Montana

PADDLING GUIDES
Floater's Guide to Colorado
Paddling Montana
Paddling Oregon

HOW-TO GUIDES
Bear Aware
Leave No Trace
Mountain Lion Alert
Wilderness First Aid
Wilderness Survival

ROCK CLIMBING GUIDES
Rock Climbing Colorado
Rock Climbing Montana
Rock Climbing New Mexico
  & Texas
Rock Climbing Utah

ROCKHOUNDING GUIDES
Rockhounding Arizona
Rockhound's Guide to California
Rockhound's Guide to Colorado
Rockhounding Montana
Rockhounding Nevada
Rockhound's Guide to New Mexico
Rockhounding Texas
Rockhounding Utah
Rockhounding Wyoming

WALKING
Walking Colorado Springs
Walking Portland
Walking St. Louis

MORE FALCONGUIDES
Backcountry Horseman's
  Guide to Washington
Camping California's
  National Forests
Exploring Canyonlands &
  Arches National Parks
Exploring Mount Helena
Recreation Guide to WA
  Nat. Forests
Touring California & Nevada
  Hot Springs
Trail Riding Western
  Montana
Wild Country Companion
Wild Montana
Wild Utah

■ *To order any of these books, check with your local bookseller or call FALCON* ® *at* ***1-800-582-2665***.

FALCON®

Visit us on the world wide web at:
www.falconguide.com